Sleepless Night

A Companion for the Dark Hours

— eloho okumo

Copyright

This book is a personal account and is not a substitute for professional medical, psychological, or legal advice.

First Edition, 2025

ISBN (eBook): 978-1-9193183-2-5
ISBN (Paperback): 978-1-9193183-0-1
ISBN (Hardcover): 978-1-9193183-1-8

Cover design: **Danish**
Interior design: **eloho**

Published by **eloho okumo**
First published in the United Kingdom

Contact: eloho@uncensoredpods.co.uk

More about my work: https://linktr.ee/elohookumo

Medical & Crisis Disclaimer & Resources

This book shares personal reflections and experiences of grief. It is not a substitute for professional medical advice, diagnosis, or treatment.

If you are struggling with your mental health, please seek support from a qualified professional such as a doctor, counsellor, or therapist. Do not disregard professional advice or delay seeking help because of something you read here.

Grief can stir emotions that feel overwhelming. If at any point you feel unsafe, unable to cope, or in crisis, please reach out immediately for support.

Immediate Crisis Support

- **United Kingdom**: Call Samaritans at 116 123 (free, 24/7)
- **United States**: Call or text 988 to connect with the Suicide & Crisis Lifeline
- **Canada**: Call or text 988 (Suicide Crisis Helpline, nationwide, 24/7)
- **South Africa**: Call SADAG Helpline at 0800 567 567 or SMS 31393 (24/7)
- **Nigeria**: Call Mentally Aware Nigeria Helpline at 0809 111 6264
- **Other African countries**: Visit findahelpline.com for local numbers.
- **International**: Visit findahelpline.com to locate support anywhere in the world.

When to Seek Help

Reach for professional support if:

- Grief feels unbearable or isolating
- You are experiencing thoughts of harming yourself
- Hallucinations, panic, or intrusive fears overwhelm you
- Daily life—sleep, eating, work, or safety—feels disrupted

You are not alone in this. Help is available.

A Gentle Note

This book speaks of loss, of sleepless nights, of panic in the dark, of hospitals and funerals, of the silence that grief leaves behind.

These words are offered with tenderness, but some pages may feel heavy.

Your well-being matters most. Read gently. Rest often. Return only when it feels safe. You are not alone here.

Some readers find it helpful to keep the Resources page marked for quick access.

When to Put This Book Down

If you are in the first days or weeks after loss, this book may feel too heavy. That is okay.

There is no wrong time to grieve, and no wrong time to read. Put this down if you need to. Come back when you are ready.

I will still be here.

Before You Begin

There is no right way to read these pages.

Dip in and out. Read in order, or let your heart choose where to begin. Pause when it feels heavy. Return when you need a hand in the dark.

Take the reflection notes and gentle prompts with you whenever the nights press hardest. Keep what comforts you. Leave what doesn't.

This book is not here to instruct. It is here to sit beside you.

Dedication

To my mum, who I lost at twenty-two.
To everyone who carries the weight of love with nowhere left to go.

To you —
Grieving in silence whilst the world moves on.
Unseen in crowded rooms, smiling whilst your heart is breaking.
Carrying questions with no answers and fears with no name.
Awake in the dark hours, wondering if this pain will ever ease.
Feeling too broken, too heavy, too much for anyone to bear.

And to you who is not yet grieving but already afraid,
lying awake thinking about the day they won't be here.
Watching someone you love grow older, fragile, or ill,
and wondering how you'll survive their absence.
Carrying the quiet dread that no one speaks about, but so many feel.

You are not morbid.
You are not broken.
You are human, and your fear is real.

And to you who has not yet lost someone, but longs to understand
how to sit beside those who have —
I see you.
I know you.
You are brave.

You are not alone in this.
May these words sit beside you
like a friend who never leaves.

Foreword

This book is not a manual, a diagnosis, or a form of professional therapy. It is a companion.

Every page is drawn from my lived experience of grief after losing my mum at twenty-two, and the years that followed. What I share here may not mirror your journey. Your grief will be your own—unpredictable, unique, deeply personal.

I do not offer prescriptions or timelines. Instead, I offer the words I once longed for—that your feelings are valid, that your reactions are not failures, and that even in the most unbearable hours, you are not alone.

If at any point you feel unsafe in your grief, or overwhelmed beyond what you can carry, I urge you to seek professional support—a counsellor, a therapist, or a trusted grief organisation. There is no weakness in asking for help. There is only courage.

This book is meant to sit beside you, not to replace the care you may need. Read it gently. Keep what comforts you. Leave what doesn't. Return whenever the nights are long.

Introduction

"Some nights are not for sleeping, but for remembering."

Grief didn't just change my inner world; it moved me across continents. I fled London for Nigeria because memory lived in every street corner—every familiar place I couldn't bear to see. And though I've since returned to London, the lessons from both continents shaped my survival.

In London, the ache was everywhere. The house was soaked in her presence—her laughter in the hallway, her footsteps on the stairs, the ordinary rhythm of life that became unbearable once it was gone. Even the streets outside—Oxford Street, the buses, the trains, the car rides we once shared—felt heavy with her absence. Every corner carried a memory I couldn't control.

In Nigeria, I thought I would be free. There were no reminders of her in the streets, no echoes of our shared routines. I told myself that if I lived somewhere new, somewhere untouched by her absence, I could start again. But grief doesn't respect geography. It followed me, seeping into unfamiliar places, unpacking itself in bedrooms and in the silence of streets that had never known her face.

What I learnt was this: *grief* is both anchor and exile. It roots you in memories you wish you could escape, and it sends you searching for places that will never be untouched enough. You can cross oceans, change continents, start over in new cities—and still, grief will arrive with you, sitting quietly in your suitcase, waiting to be unpacked again.

This book is not a story of moving on, because I never did. It is a companion for anyone awake in the dark hours, when loss feels unbearable and silence feels too loud—and for the ordinary daylight hours too, when grief quietly shadows the rhythm of daily life.

It is for those who are grieving—who wake each day trying to live with what's gone.

It is for those who sense loss approaching—whether it's a parent growing older, a loved one fading, or someone you cannot imagine life without—who find themselves imagining that moment before it arrives, wondering how they will survive it.

And it is for those standing beside someone in grief—who may not know what to say, but wish to understand how to be there, gently and truthfully.

If this is you, you are not alone. The fear of loss, the ache of absence, the helplessness of witnessing pain—all of it is part of being human. Many people carry these quiet weights but rarely speak about them.

Loss comes for all of us. That isn't pessimism; it's reality. Preparing your heart for it doesn't invite tragedy—it invites readiness. It invites the chance to notice what matters now, whilst you still can.

When my mum died, I realised how much I hadn't saved—her voice, her laughter, the photos and videos I thought I'd always have time to take. I thought I had decades. I didn't. If you still have time, this book will remind you not to wait. And if loss has already arrived, it will sit with you in the aftermath.

Here you will find fragments—stories, reflections, questions, and small rituals. Some are raw, born in the first season of grief when I was twenty-two and everything had just shattered. Others were written later, in the second season I'm still living through: quieter, but just as heavy, teaching me that grief never leaves; it only changes shape.

I was twenty-two when grief first found me. Now, in my thirties, I understand it differently—and this book is for anyone, at any age, still learning how to live with loss.

If you are holding this book, it is not to find answers but to feel less alone. Grief isolates—it convinces you that your experience is strange, unbearable, unshareable. But here is the truth: you are not strange. You are not unbearable. You are not alone.

These words are not instruction. They are presence—the companion I wish I had at twenty-two, the voice that might have said: *You are not broken. This chaos is love, learning how to live in a world that has changed forever.*

So let's walk together—through sleepless nights and the hours when fear has no name, through the strange language of grief, surviving in public while falling apart, and discovering who stays, who goes, and who surprises you. Through the changing shapes of love, the loneliness lie, the silence of faith, and the oceans we cross to outrun memory. Through anticipatory grief and the call to say it now, before it's too late. Through envy and regret, through rituals that anchor, through the quiet return of purpose and the second seasons that follow. Through the bridges that carry us forward, the reclamations that remake us, and the lives grief builds, again and again.

Author's Note

These pages are not from a healed place, but from an honest one.

"I cannot take your grief away, but I will sit with you in it."

Table of Contents

COMPANION TOOLS

CLOSING

If You Need a Companion

This book is not meant to be read in order.
If you're in crisis, use this guide to find the chapter you need.

If you're feeling:

Crisis support numbers are listed at the front and back of this book.

Chapter One

7 July, 1 PM

"Grief doesn't announce itself. It arrives on ordinary days and rewrites the story you thought you were living."

The Bathroom

It was the bathroom where everything ended.

7 July, 2012—a Saturday afternoon, around 1 PM. I had been up all night talking on the phone to my best friend, the way you do when you're twenty-two and the world still feels like it belongs to you. I finally drifted off around three, heavy with laughter and youth, certain that tomorrow would be ordinary.

Then I woke up to it. My mum's scream.

"elohoooo!"

The sound tore through the stillness like a blade. I bolted upright, heart pounding, and ran to the living room—empty. I turned towards the bathroom. That's where I found her.

She was crumpled against the bathtub, her body rigid, her breath coming in short, torn gasps that sounded like drowning. Her eyes were shut, her face strained, exposed and vulnerable on the cold floor.

I dropped to my knees and screamed, "Mum! Mum!" But then my body betrayed me. Fear rooted me to the spot. I froze, convinced that what I was seeing wasn't survivable.

I bolted for the phone and dialled the ambulance first, nearly dropping it in my panic. Then I called my brother Timi. He didn't pick up. I tried Tony next. Still no answer. My hands were trembling. Finally, I called my cousin Jenny, my words breaking apart as I tried to explain.

Jenny was at home with Tare and her mum, my Auntie Gifty. They didn't wait. They hailed a black cab immediately and rushed to my house.

But I didn't go back. I didn't kneel beside her. I didn't hold her hand or whisper, "Mum, breathe. I'm here."

Instead, I paced the hallway like an animal trapped. My legs refused to carry me back to her.

I stood outside, praying to God. Not because I was particularly religious, but because I was raised that way—and because some part of me knew this was bad. Really bad.

The night before, she had teased me through my bedroom door while I whispered into the phone at 3 AM. She knew it was a boy, even though he was just my best friend.

"Who are you talking to, eloho?" she'd laughed, her voice playful and insistent.

I groaned, dragged the covers over my head, and shouted back, "Mum, leave me alone."

I didn't know that would be the last time she called my name in laughter before she called it in terror.

"God, please help my mum. My mum shall live. Lord, please help my mum."

The words spilled out in loops, as if repetition could bargain with reality.

Going to the Hospital

"The distance I can never close"

The ambulance arrived. There wasn't space for all of us, so Jenny, Tare, Auntie Gifty, and I took a black cab to St Thomas' Hospital whilst the ambulance took my mum.

I should have insisted on riding with her. They were still doing CPR, still fighting to bring her back. But I let them take her without me. I got into the black cab instead, leaving her alone in that ambulance with strangers.

Even now, thirteen years later, I regret that choice. I should have been there. Holding her hand. Whispering that I was with her. But I wasn't. I was in a cab, racing behind, whilst she fought for her life without me.

By the time we arrived at the hospital, they were still working on her. It had taken them a while to get there—maybe if I'd been in the ambulance, if I'd been there...

But I wasn't.

The Corridor

"The words no child should hear"

At the hospital, Jenny and I were on our way to the bathroom when I leaned close and whispered, "This is bad, Jenny. This is really bad."

She hushed me, told me not to think negatively. On our way back through the corridor, she was still urging me to stay positive, still telling me not to expect the worst. But my gut has always been sharp. Deby, one of my closest friends, often said I sensed when things were wrong before anyone else. This time my whole body was already screaming.

When my aunties arrived, one of them looked straight at me and, instead of comfort, gave me blame. "*eloho, what have you done*?" she snapped, as if I had conjured my mother's collapse myself. In our culture, crisis often demands someone to blame. Fear makes people cruel, and grief needs an outlet. But her words pierced me like a second knife.

It was during that walk back from the bathroom, just as my feet carried me into the corridor, that the doctor delivered the words no child is ever prepared to hear.

My mum had died.

The floor gave way. My knees buckled. Jenny and Tare caught me as I fell, holding me upright whilst my body collapsed.

I stumbled outside, desperate for air, but found only despair. The street blurred. Jenny and Tare stood beside me, probably thinking, *My God, her mum is gone. What do we do?*

But I wasn't thinking about them. I was thinking: *What if I just ran into it? Let the bus hit me. Let me follow her. Let me escape this life that had become unrecognisable in a single breath.*

I needed to die. I didn't want to live. Why should I be here when she wasn't? In my head, the plan formed quickly—run. Step into the road. Let the bus hit me. But Jenny and Tare were right there. If I moved, they'd catch me. So I went quiet, silent on the outside while chaos screamed inside, standing still and calculating the right moment in my mind.

That's when Seun appeared. My friend. My anchor in that instant. Her presence pulled me back from the edge, distracted me from the plan forming in my head. In that moment, her existence kept me alive.

Coming Home

"The silence that followed"

I don't remember how I got home. I don't know who drove me. The timeline of that day dissolved the moment she died.

What I do remember is sitting on my bed, staring into emptiness. Not at the wall. Not at anything specific. Just... emptiness. The air itself felt different, like the atmosphere had changed and I was breathing something foreign.

My friends were there—voices around me, concerned faces. But I wasn't present in my own body. I was somewhere else entirely, watching the scene happen to someone who looked like me.

Then my brother Tony came in. He'd been at the hospital with me. Timi, my older brother, had stayed back at the hospital, he hadn't come with us. Tony needed to know what happened. Needed me to tell him the story whilst it was still fresh.

So I relived it. "I was sleeping. I slept late. Then I heard my name—*elohooo*—and I woke up and ran to the living room and she wasn't there, so I checked the bathroom, and I saw her on the floor..."

He asked the question I'd been asking myself: "Why didn't you just drive her to St Thomas' Hospital? Why wait for the ambulance? The hospital's just around the corner. We live in Pimlico."

I tried to explain. "I was scared. I was confused. I don't know if I could have lifted her by myself, put clothes on her. I don't know what I was doing."

"You could have tried," he said.

"I know," I whispered. "I know."

The truth was, I'd only recently passed my driving test. I wasn't confident behind the wheel. The fear had paralysed me. But more than that, I'd failed her. In the moment she needed me most, I'd run to the hallway instead of staying by her side. I'd called for help instead of being the help she needed.

I didn't feel defensive when Tony asked those questions. How could I? They were the same questions screaming in my own head. If he had been the one in that hallway, paralysed with the phone to his ear and unable to return to the bathroom that day, I would've asked him the same thing. *Why didn't you just do it?*

But talking about it now, thirteen years later, the defensiveness rises. Because reliving it means reliving the neglect—the moment I abandoned her when she was drowning on dry land.

Jenny's House

"Noise became a lifeline"

I couldn't sleep in that house. Not in my room. Not anywhere near the bathroom where I'd found her.

So I took my things to my cousin Jenny's house. Not just Jenny—her whole family. My mum's sister, other cousins. A home full of noise and talking and life. That noise saved me. If I'd been alone, I would have gone mad.

I stayed there for months, until around October—maybe longer, until I moved to Soho. Being in someone else's space, surrounded by family, helped save my life. The alternative, being alone with my thoughts in that house, would have destroyed me.

But even at Jenny's, even surrounded by family, I couldn't escape her.

Every time I closed my eyes, I saw my mum's face. Not reminiscing—seeing. Her face from the bathroom. Her face in the hospital bed. Every version of her face I could recall, appearing the moment I tried to rest. All those thoughts racing: not holding her hand, not being there, not rushing her to the hospital myself.

It wasn't memory. It was hallucination. Traumatising. Terrifying.

And then came the fear: if I closed my eyes, I would die. If I fell asleep, I wouldn't wake up.

That fear lasted for over a year—maybe longer. And here's the truth: thirteen years later, I still have it. Not as strong, but still there. Even now, I sometimes think, *What if I sleep and don't wake up?*

I've even made peace with it in a strange way. I always say my preferred way to die is to sleep and not wake up—peaceful, no struggle, just gone.

But in the beginning, that fear was absolute. For over a year, I didn't sleep at night. I couldn't. Darkness felt like death waiting. I only slept once daylight came, once I felt safe again.

Everything scared me in those months: the dark, being alone, going out by myself. And bathrooms—especially bathrooms. Even visiting my brothers at my mum's house later, I'd stand in the bathroom doorway thinking, *This is where it happened. This is where she fell. Will I fall too? Will I just collapse and die?* Looking in the mirror, seeing it all reflected back. Every time I went in there, I was petrified.

That's when my series addiction was born. I needed something to fill the dark hours, something to keep my mind occupied whilst the world slept. I watched series every day—like breathing, like eating, like surviving.

Even now, thirteen years later, I watch them daily. They're the only thing that quiets the fear, the memories, the absence. Only my work—the podcast, this book, the Kit—can pull me away. Otherwise, series are my constant companion. My survival mechanism that never left.

The Funeral

"Seeing what I couldn't unsee"

I had no contribution to the funeral. I couldn't.
Remember, I was twenty-two— the youngest. Death wasn't part of my vocabulary. The only time I'd ever spoken of death was in prayers: *"I shall not die; I shall live long."* That's what Christians say. That's what I believed.

I didn't know death was real. I didn't know it could happen to *her*.

My brothers handled the arrangements. Maybe I helped find funeral directors once. Maybe. But I wasn't telling people how to bury my mum, what to wear, or what hymns to sing. I just listened, nodded, agreed.

I kept asking Timi, "Are you sure she's dead?"

He'd look at me, patient, broken. "Yes."

"But... she's not going to wake up?"

"No, eloho. She's not."

I never went to see her body at the mortuary. I couldn't. In my head, she wasn't dead. She couldn't be.

But on the day of the funeral, one of my aunties—someone I barely knew—decided I needed to do a final viewing.

"eloho, you have to see her one last time before we leave," she said.

"No. I'm not doing that."

"You have to. You have to."

She pulled me. Physically pulled me into the room where my mum's body lay.

I looked.

And what I saw didn't look like my mum. Her face was dark, decayed, unrecognisable. That was not my mother.

I ran. Just turned and ran out of that room, terrified and shaking.

The auntie said something—maybe that it was good to look, maybe that it was fine if I couldn't. I don't remember. I only remember that face that wasn't hers, and the terror of realising she was truly, irreversibly gone.

That image tried to replace every good memory I had of her. For years, when I thought of my mum, that's what I saw first. It took time—so much time—to push it back, to choose to remember her in that hospital bed instead, her face still soft, still hers.

I tried going back to her grave. Two, maybe three times. The last time, something changed. That night, panic attacks began. My body rebelled against the reality I could no longer deny. Since then, I've never returned. The cemetery became the birthplace of my terror—the line between presence and absence too sharp to cross again.

The Beginning of After

"The work of survival begins"

Shock is a mercy. My body knew I couldn't process everything at once, so it shut down parts of my mind to protect me.

Asking "Are you sure she's dead?" wasn't denial—it was my heart trying to make sense of the impossible.

Hallucinations and fear of sleep are normal responses to trauma. My body was trying to process what my mind couldn't hold.

Noise and company became survival tools. My cousin's home kept me tethered to life when isolation would have destroyed me.

Series weren't escapism—they were anchors, filling the unbearable silence when nothing else could.

Some images, like that final viewing, can haunt you for years. But you can learn to choose which memories to hold closest.

Most importantly, the immediate aftermath of loss is pure chaos. There's no right way to respond, no proper way to grieve, no perfect way to survive. You just do whatever keeps you breathing until the next moment arrives.

For You, If You've Just Begun

What do you remember most clearly from the day you lost them—and what has time blurred?

If you froze or ran when they needed you, have you found a way to forgive yourself?

Who became your safe person in those first impossible days?

What small thing kept you breathing when everything else felt impossible?

The Work of Survival

"The breaking doesn't happen in one moment. It's the bathroom floor, the hospital corridor, the sleepless nights, the hallucinations, the unanswerable questions. It's every small shattering that follows the first—until you realise: survival itself has become the work."

Chapter Two

When Fear Had No Name

"Panic is grief showing up in your body."

I didn't know what panic attacks were when they first came for me.

For three months after my mum died, I lived in a different kind of terror—the hallucinations, the sleepless nights, the constant fear that closing my eyes meant never waking up. But I hadn't yet experienced what would become my body's loudest language for grief.

That changed the night I returned from visiting her grave.

I was alone in my room in Soho when my chest suddenly clamped shut. My breath turned shallow and quick, as though I was drowning. My heart hammered so violently I could hear it in my ears, convinced it would explode or simply stop altogether.

I paced the small room, clutching my chest, whispering desperately to myself: *Am I dying? Is this it? Is this how it ends for me too?*

The terror was absolute. It wasn't just fear—it was the bone-deep certainty that death was coming for me in that exact moment. My hands shook uncontrollably. Sweat broke across my skin despite the cool evening. The walls felt as though they were pressing in, making the room smaller with every panicked breath.

I had no language for what was happening—no framework to understand why my body was betraying me when my mind was trying so hard to hold things together. The not-knowing made everything worse. When you can't name something, it owns you completely.

That was the last time I went back to her grave. The cemetery should have been a place of remembrance, but for me it became the trigger that awakened terror in my body. From then on, the panic followed me everywhere: into bedrooms, buses, quiet moments alike.

Grief had found a new language—it spoke through my chest, my breath, my trembling hands.

Most times the attacks came at night, jerking me awake with my heart already racing. Other times they ambushed me during the day: in the middle of a conversation, whilst buying groceries, or simply sitting quietly. There was no pattern I could predict, no trigger I could avoid. They arrived like storms—sudden and devastating.

The worst part was the isolation. How do you explain to someone that your body is screaming danger when you're sitting safely in your own room? How do you describe the sensation of drowning whilst breathing, of dying whilst living?

I started calling Joy in the middle of these episodes. She was the first friend I'd made after moving from Nigeria to the UK, and somehow she became the person I trusted with my terror.

At 2 AM, shaking and certain I was about to die, I would call her.

"Something's happening to me," I would whisper into the phone. "I don't know what it is, but I think I'm dying."

Joy never hesitated. "Come over," she'd say simply.

I would take an Uber to her house, trembling in the back seat, watching the city blur past through tear-filled eyes. When I arrived, she would open the door without questions, let me crawl into her bed, and simply stay.

My body didn't calm—the panic still rattled through me like a trapped animal—but I felt safe. Safe in the only way that mattered: if death did come, at least I wouldn't be alone.

Joy's mum worried about me too. *"Make sure you open the door for her,"* she would tell Joy. *"Stay awake until she's safely inside."*

Their family welcomed me like their own, covering me in the places I couldn't cover myself.

For months I lived in this nameless terror. Each attack convinced me something was fundamentally wrong—with my heart, my lungs, my entire system. I started avoiding situations that might trigger whatever this was, which meant avoiding almost everything. Grief had already stolen my mother; now this unknown thing was stealing my life.

Finally, Joy said the words that changed everything: *Go to the GP.*

The doctor was matter-of-fact—that felt like salvation. After I described the racing heart, the breathlessness, the overwhelming certainty of death, she looked at me calmly and said:

"You are having panic attacks."

Three words that gave me back my sanity.

She explained how grief can hijack the nervous system, how the body processes trauma in ways the mind doesn't understand. She taught me breathing exercises—in for four counts, hold for four, out for six. She showed me how to slow my racing heart by placing cold water on my wrists, how to ground myself by naming what I could see and touch.

It didn't stop the panic attacks immediately, but it gave me something precious: language.

When you can name your demon, it loses some of its power over you. What had felt like madness or medical emergency was actually my body's way of processing the unthinkable loss of my mother.

The attacks still come sometimes, even now, thirteen years later. But they no longer feel like death sentences. I know what they are. I know they will pass. I know the difference between my body remembering trauma and my body actually being in danger.

If you're reading this in the grip of nameless terror, know this: what you're experiencing has a name—and having a name means it can be understood.

Your body isn't broken. It's carrying a weight your heart can't hold alone. The fear is real, but it isn't forever.

When the Body Became a Messenger

"The body remembers what the mind can't say"

Placing both hands on my chest and saying it out loud helped: *This is panic, not danger. My body is remembering, not dying.*

Counting breaths worked—in for four, hold for four, out for six. Doing this ten times, focusing only on the numbers, helped ground me.

The 5-4-3 technique pulled me back: five things I could see, four I could touch, three I could hear. My senses anchored me to the present moment.

Cold water became my friend—running it over my wrists, splashing it on my face, or holding an ice cube. Cold shocks the nervous system back to calm.

Having one person I could text or call during an attack made all the difference: *I'm having panic. Can you stay on the phone with me?*

Most importantly, this truth: every panic attack I've survived has ended. The next one will too.

For You, If Fear Still Speaks Through Your Body

What does your body feel like just before panic begins—tight chest, racing thoughts, sweaty palms?

Who is your safe person to call when fear has no name and everything feels like an emergency?

What words would you want a doctor to say to you in your most terrified moment?

Your Superpower

"Fear may visit without warning, but it always leaves. You are not your panic. You are the person who survives it, again and again. Some days you'll barely notice its arrival. Other days it will flatten you. But every single time, you will outlast it. That's not weakness. That's your superpower."

Chapter Three

When Sleep Becomes the Enemy

"Night is when grief takes off its mask."

The days were brutal, but the nights were worse. When the noise faded, when no one was calling, when the world finally went quiet, that's when grief grew loudest.

Even when the panic eased, the nights never did. They stayed wide open, endless, reminding me that grief doesn't end when the heartbeat slows.

Sleep became impossible. My body refused it, my mind fought it, and my chest carried the kind of dread that only came alive at 2 AM.

I would lie in bed staring at the ceiling, heart pounding, the silence broken only by the sound of my own shallow breathing. My phone would glow beside me. I scrolled endlessly, desperate for distraction, watching strangers live lives I couldn't reach. Other nights, I paced the floor in circles, whispering to myself just to fill the air.

The hours between midnight and morning stretched into eternity. By dawn, I would collapse into sleep—not restful, not healing, just exhaustion knocking me out for a few hours. Then I'd wake to another day I didn't want to face.

Anchors in the Darkness

"When sleep abandoned me, I went searching for substitutes"

My series addiction began in Soho, where silence filled the nights. Endless episodes on loop, borrowed lives filling the void. Fiction was a shield. If I could drown in someone else's story, maybe I could escape my own.

Running and the gym, which Yasmina had introduced me to years before, became more than the anchors they'd been in those first months. When I ran, the world went quiet: just breath, pavement, heartbeat, and the music in my ears. There was effort, but also release—a fleeting sense of weight lifting off me, even if only for a mile or two.

I would drag myself to the gym, eyes heavy, muscles aching, because movement was the only thing that reminded me I was still alive. It was exhaustion on purpose. If I could empty my body completely, maybe, just maybe, it would let me sleep. Most nights it didn't work. But I kept going anyway, because at least it was something I could control.

Some nights I'd keep a lamp on so the dark couldn't swallow me whole. Sometimes I'd call Joy, who still answered at 3 AM without hesitation, her voice the only thread tying me back to the world.

Other nights, I'd put on music just loud enough to drown out the silence. Or I'd hold something physical—a pillow, my Teddy. Each gesture was a quiet reach for her. Small things tethered me to her, to myself, to living.

It wasn't healing. It was survival. And in those nights, survival was enough.

The Night's Quiet Debt

People think grief is loudest at funerals, birthdays, anniversaries. But for me, the battlefield was always night. Darkness magnified everything: every fear, every regret, every unanswered question.

I had to be indoors before it got dark, especially in winter. The evening felt heavy, the shadows stretching longer with every minute. My body learned to anticipate disaster even when nothing was happening. The smallest sound—a siren, an ambulance passing—was enough to send me spiralling.

Sometimes the silence was worse than any sound, pressing into my ears, my chest, my skin, reminding me of what I had lost and what I feared might happen next.

At night it was often worse, as if the darkness pulled my mother's voice from the past and pressed it into the present. I could hear her screaming my name, and my nervous system remembered every inch of it. The memory of that sound lingered long after, shaping how I felt in every quiet, dark moment that followed.

The Silence That Kept Me Awake

The night is not proof of weakness: it's proof of love. Sleeplessness is what happens when grief has nowhere to go—when love rattles the cage of your chest because it can't find the person it belongs to.

The night magnifies everything—memories, regrets, unfinished words—but it can also hold you if you let it.

Small anchors can steady you: a voice note from a friend, a lamp left on, a series running quietly in the background until dawn. The goal isn't sleep. The goal is survival—making it to morning without being swallowed whole.

For You, If the Nights Still Stretch Too Long

What makes the night feel heavier than the day?

What anchors can you reach for when silence turns dangerous?

What ritual, however small, might remind you that you are not alone?

Love in the Dark

"Your sleeplessness is not failure. It is love keeping vigil. The dark hours may feel endless, but you are still here."

Chapter Four

The Strange Language of Grief

"You are not broken. The strange things you feel are grief's language in your body."

Nobody warned me how strange grief would feel—I thought it was only sadness, tears, and missing my mum. But grief is sneaky. It shows up in your body, in your thoughts, and in the most unexpected places, speaking a language I'd never learned but was suddenly forced to understand.

After the initial shock of 7 July, after learning to name my panic attacks and survive the sleepless nights, grief began speaking through my body in ways that made me question my sanity.

When Words Disappeared

There were days I forgot the simplest words, standing mid-sentence with my mouth open, grasping for vocabulary that had simply vanished. I would walk into a room and stand there completely lost, staring at familiar walls as if I'd never seen them before.

Grief fog is real—as if someone had unplugged my brain and plugged it back in halfway. Concentration became impossible. Memory turned unreliable. Even language itself, something I'd never questioned, became foreign territory where words hid from me when I needed them most.

I went to the doctor, worried something was wrong. They said I was fine. But I knew better. Grief was inside me, and my body remembered what my mind tried desperately to forget.

The Weight Only I Could Feel

Then there were the physical anchors grief dropped into my body. My chest felt heavy, as though someone had placed a stone there whilst I slept and forgotten to remove it. My shoulders carried an invisible weight, like unseen hands pressing down. Some mornings I woke with my entire body trembling, as though I'd been crying all night without knowing.

Time itself became distorted. I would blink and entire months had vanished, slipping away without leaving any trace in my memory. Yet a five-minute silence could stretch endlessly, every second crawling by like torture. Grief makes you feel both frozen and rushed, as though life is happening around you whilst you remain trapped in slow motion.

And then there were the moments that made me question reality—thinking I heard my mum's voice calling from the kitchen, expecting her name to light up my phone screen, feeling a phantom touch on my shoulder as if she'd just walked up behind me.

Sometimes these moments comforted me, like gentle visitations from somewhere beyond. Other times they felt cruel—sharp reminders that she was not coming back, that my mind was playing tricks my heart couldn't bear.

Oxford Street

"The day I chased a ghost in daylight"

One afternoon, months after she died, I was walking down Oxford Street when I saw her.

My heart stopped. There she was: the same walk, the same posture, the same way of carrying herself. Everything about this woman screamed my mum.

I ran. Actually ran, weaving through the Saturday crowd, my bag banging against my hip, people turning to stare. I didn't care. She was right there, just ahead of me, walking away like she always did when I was slow to keep up.

"*Mum*! *Mum*!" I called out, my voice breaking, louder each time. "*Mum, wait*!"

The woman turned.

Confused. Alarmed. A stranger's face.

It wasn't her. Of course it wasn't her.

I stood there frozen, breathless, the crowd moving around me like I was a stone in a river. The woman looked at me with a mixture of concern and fear, probably wondering if I was dangerous, if she should run.

"*Sorry*," I whispered. Then louder: "*Sorry, sorry, so sorry*."

Embarrassment flooded me first. Then fresh grief, crashing over me in waves right there on Oxford Street. People glanced, then looked away quickly—the way strangers do when they witness someone breaking in public.

I thought I was going crazy. Losing my grip on reality itself. How could I have been so certain? How could my brain have betrayed me so completely, turning a stranger into the person I missed most in the world?

I don't remember how I got home that day. Just that when I did, I crawled into bed fully dressed and stayed there until the next morning, replaying that moment over and over—the running, the calling, the turning, the stranger's face that wasn't hers.

It wasn't the last time I mistook someone for her. But it was the worst. The most public. The most undeniable proof that grief was reshaping my reality, making me see what I desperately wanted to see, even when it wasn't there.

Just as my body began to adjust, the world demanded something colder—paperwork.

The Bureaucracy of Loss

No one prepares you for the paperwork of death. The heart is broken, yet the world demands signatures, forms, proof. Suddenly you are a grieving daughter and administrator at once.

I remember waiting to sign the documents for my mum. My brothers handled the calls, the arrangements, the endless logistics. I was there to sign, to witness, to follow along as needed. I held the piece of paper that felt heavier than anything I had ever carried. My hands shook so badly I could barely sign.

Letters blurred. Deadlines loomed. Grief drains the body, and bureaucracy doesn't care. Cancel the bank account. Notify insurance. Sign forms that sound cold and sterile but cut like knives. Every call, every form, every tick-box whispered the same brutal truth:

She is gone.

Paperwork is not just paperwork. It is grief translated into tasks the world demands, and love showing up in signatures they can no longer write. Love doesn't end with death; it signs the forms, makes the calls, carries the weight.

When Reality Bent and Broke

Keeping a grief diary helped me track sleep, brain fog, and physical aches. Seeing patterns made the unknown less frightening.

When my chest felt heavy, I learned to place both palms there and breathe slowly. The weight would soften, just a little.

Brain fog forced me to write everything down—lists, reminders, even the smallest tasks. I let paper carry what memory couldn't.

Gentle movement helped more than I expected: a walk, a stretch, ten minutes of sunlight. My body needed to remember it was alive.

Staying hydrated mattered. Grief dehydrates more than you realise.

When I mistook a stranger for my mum, I had to pause and breathe. My mind was searching for her. It hurt, but it wasn't madness.

For You, If the World Feels Unreal

What is the strangest physical or mental shift you've noticed since your loss?

How does your body carry what your heart cannot say?

When time feels distorted, what helps you feel present again?

Which rituals—tea, stretching, journalling—remind your body it is still safe?

Have you ever mistaken a stranger for them? How did you recover from that moment?

Fluent in Love

"Grief speaks in a dialect you never wanted to learn. But learning it doesn't make you fluent in madness—it makes you fluent in love that has nowhere to go."

Chapter Five

Surviving in Public While Falling Apart

"When the world expects normal, showing up is already brave."

Grief doesn't stay at home. It follows you everywhere: into classrooms, into shops, into crowded buses—like an unwelcome shadow. From the outside, I might have looked "fine." But inside, everything ordinary took ten times more energy. A single question—*How are you?*—felt like an exam I hadn't studied for.

Three weeks after my mum died, I went back to university. I sat in lectures about television production while my mind replayed the sound of her last breaths. Around me, people scribbled notes on narrative structure; I was just trying to stop my chest from caving in.

The hardest part wasn't even the grief itself: it was the performance. Smiling when people looked at me. Nodding in conversations I couldn't hear. Handing in essays that took me three times longer because I had to stop, again and again, just to breathe.

Simple things turned into mountains. Buying groceries meant landmines: her favourite tea, the biscuits she always bought, the smell of washing powder that still clung to her clothes at home. Standing in line felt unbearable—certain my grief was loud enough for everyone to hear.

Work With a Hollow Core

Work wasn't any easier. I had a retail job, and grief clocked in beside me every day.

One afternoon, a customer asked where the fitting rooms were. I heard her voice but couldn't make the words connect to meaning. She asked again. Then a third time—irritation creeping in.

My coworker stepped in: "I'll show you." Then, quieter, to me: "Take five. Go to the stockroom."

I walked to the back, hands on my knees, staring at stacks of boxes, trying to remember how to be a person who could give simple directions. The lights buzzed overhead. My breath came shallow. I counted to ten, then twenty, then back to one.

Eventually I stood up, smoothed my shirt, and returned to the floor. No one asked what was wrong, and I was grateful for that.

Sometimes silence is mercy.

The Graduation That Wasn't

October came—graduation day, just months after 7 July.

I didn't want to go. How could I? What was there to celebrate without her? My brother, Timi, insisted: "You worked too hard not to walk that stage."

So I dressed, put on the gown, painted myself in enough composure to pass.

But the moment I arrived, I unravelled. Everywhere I looked, mothers were adjusting gowns, crying proud tears, pulling their children in for photographs. My body burned with absence.

I slipped away before the ceremony ended. No official photo. No smiling memory to mark the day. Just a hollow ache wearing a gown.

Bus 24 to Oxford Street

One afternoon, I boarded a packed bus, trying to act normal. I stood gripping the rail, surrounded by chatter and headphones. Out of nowhere, my chest tightened and I couldn't breathe. My eyes blurred, my body trembling as strangers pressed around me.

I wanted to scream: *My mum just died. Please, someone, see me.* But I said nothing.

I got off two stops early, collapsed onto a bench, and sobbed into my hands whilst London carried on around me. Nobody asked if I was okay. That silence cut almost as much as the grief itself.

I sat on that bench for what felt like hours but was probably twenty minutes. People passed. Some glanced. Most didn't. Eventually, I went home and crawled into bed with my shoes still on, letting the world continue without me.

Sometimes that's all the grief allows you: a small pause, a place to collapse, and nothing more.

Fluent in Disguise

That's the loneliness no one warns you about. You can be surrounded by people who love you and still feel utterly alone. They didn't know it had taken me an hour to get dressed because I'd cried in the shower. To them, I looked like eloho.

But I wasn't. I was carrying an impossible weight whilst the world demanded productivity and smiles. It wasn't pretending: it was surviving. It was becoming fluent in grief's disguise.

When Words Failed Me

I began to realise I couldn't give the world perfect composure. What I owed was protection—choosing where to spend the little energy I had.

So I started using tiny phrases that told the truth without giving everything away.

To a manager: "I'm managing a bereavement; my capacity is reduced."

To friends: "I want to come, but I may leave early."

Those sentences became shields—small ways of protecting myself from a world that kept expecting too much.

Leaving early without apology became necessary. Letting someone else carry the conversation. Having one or two steady allies close: people who could bridge the gap between me and the noise when I couldn't speak for myself.

On my heaviest days, survival was the only job. Nothing else.

There will always be people who don't understand—and that is about their limits, not my worth. Measuring energy like currency, choosing where to spend it, and saving what I could for myself became acts of self-preservation.

For You, If Words Have Stopped Making Sense

How do you carry grief when the world expects you to act "normal"?

What small actions or words help you protect your energy in public?

When grief hits unexpectedly in everyday spaces, how do you give yourself permission to pause?

Have you noticed moments when your body reacts before your mind can catch up? How do you respond?

Bravery in the Small Things

"Some days, showing up is the only triumph"

"You don't have to perform normal. Just standing in the room, carrying this ache, is braver than anyone knows. And some days, just making it from your bed to the front door is the entire victory."

Chapter Six

Who Stays, Who Goes, Who Surprises You

"Grief rearranges your friendships. Some drift, some stay, some arrive as lifelines."

When my mum died at twenty-two—I thought my friends would instinctively know what to do. I imagined calls that lasted hours, visits that stretched deep into the night, someone sitting beside me until the panic passed or the sun rose—whichever came first. I thought they would read my silence the way my mum once did, understanding the language of my grief before I even knew how to speak it myself.

Some did. Many didn't. And their silence felt louder than any words ever could.

At first, I mistook that silence for abandonment: for concrete proof that I didn't matter as much as I'd thought I did. I told myself they didn't care, that our friendships had been built on shallow ground that couldn't survive real tragedy. The anger felt easier than the hurt, so I wrapped myself in it like protective armour.

With time, I learned that silence often comes from fear—fear of saying the wrong thing, of making the pain worse; of confronting their own discomfort with death and loss. None of it erased the sting, but it helped me see that their silence was about their limitations, not my worth. It took time to stop measuring love by presence alone.

Grief rearranges your friendships with surgical precision. Some people drift away, unable to sit with the heaviness you now carry everywhere. Some step closer, drawn by an instinct to protect and comfort. Some surprise you completely: acquaintances become lifelines, family friends open their doors without hesitation, parents of friends offer their homes when yours feels too empty to bear.

And as much as it hurts to lose people, it also makes the ones who stay stand out with brilliant clarity. Silence reveals who can sit in the dark with you, even when they don't have the right words to fill it.

The hardest lesson is that no single person can carry your grief. One friend may sit quietly beside you. Another may distract you with laughter when tears feel impossible. Another may disappear altogether, leaving you wondering if they ever really knew you at all. Each absence wounds, but each presence—however small or imperfect—matters more than you can possibly know in the moment.

Silence can wound, but it can also teach you to recognise the quieter forms of love that often hide beneath the noise.

Friends Who Became My Compass

Esse: The Mirror of Truth

"Sometimes love was there all along, just not in the language I was listening for"

I've known Esse for over twenty years—one of my oldest and dearest friends. She knew my mum well. Before I relocated to the UK, when my mum would visit Nigeria, Esse would sleep beside us in the hotel room—the three of us tucked into one bed, laughter spilling into the night. When my mum couldn't reach me, she called Esse. That's how close we are. She isn't just my friend: she is family.

Not long after my mum died, I fled London for Nigeria—chasing air I thought would be easier to breathe. That was when I expected Esse to move in with me, to stay for as long as it took for the world to stop spinning. In my mind, she would live with me, carry me through every dark hour, every panic attack, and fill the silence my mother left behind.

But grief made me unreasonable. I wanted her near even when I wasn't kind. My pain was loud and unpredictable, and sometimes she met the sharp edge of it. Looking back now, I can see that I made the room too heavy for her, or anyone, to stay in. So when she left, I felt abandoned—but I understand now that she was protecting her peace, not punishing me.

Esse showed up in her own way. Maybe not every hour, maybe not always in the language I wanted, but her care was steady. I was too consumed by my expectations to recognise that love was still there—quieter, gentler, and different from what I imagined.

Years later, during the pandemic, on Clubhouse—in one of those late-night rooms—I found myself saying, *"Esse, you weren't there for me when my mum died."* My voice was sharper than I meant, too loud, too certain, spilling years of misplaced anger into the open. She didn't defend herself. She stayed silent. And somehow, that silence said everything.

After we left the call, I sat with it. I replayed my own words, hearing how cruel they sounded. Eight years had passed—from losing my mum in 2012, to relocating to Nigeria in 2013, and now here we were in 2020—and still, I was carrying that wound as if no time had passed at all. I knew I'd embarrassed her. I knew Esse doesn't like being spoken to that way. That realisation hit hard.

An hour later, I called her privately to apologise. That call became a turning point. I realised then that she had been there all along: picking up when I called, holding space quietly, loving me through the chaos I created. Sometimes it takes years, even decades, for clarity to arrive. But when it does, it humbles you. It reminds you that love was never absent—only unseen.

There were moments that proved it long before I understood. Once, during one of my sleepless nights, I called Esse, terrified and unable to calm my body. I told her, "You have to stay on the phone with me until I fall asleep." And she did. We fell asleep on the call together. That's who she's always been—steady, gentle, quietly present in the background, never making noise about her care, just showing up when it mattered.

If you've ever looked at a friend through the fog of pain and thought they weren't there for you, pause. Look again. Sometimes love comes quietly—not in grand gestures, but in the soft persistence of someone who still answers your call. And when clarity returns, let grace lead you to the words: *I'm sorry.* I see you now. Apologies don't undo pain, but they create space for healing—for both of you.

Esse is still in my life today. Just recently, whilst visiting London after a holiday, she shared her own loss—the passing of a close friend. It reminded me that grief eventually visits everyone, and that our friendship has carried us both through storms we couldn't have faced alone.

After all these years, we no longer need constant contact to feel close. Ours is a friendship that breathes: stretching, pausing, but never breaking. Proof that love can bend beneath the weight of grief and still hold.

"Love that endures isn't the loudest—it's the one that stays, quietly holding on long after the noise fades."

The Apology Tour

"Grief doesn't only break your heart; sometimes it breaks your manners too"

In the years after my mum died, I went on what I now call my apology tour.

I reached out to people I'd hurt—people I'd snapped at, dismissed, shut out when they were only trying to help. Some had offered comfort and I'd thrown it back in their faces. Others had simply been in my path when the rage boiled over, and they became collateral damage.

I remember one particular moment that still makes me cringe. Deby had surprised me one day, saying she was just taking me out. She picked me up from my house, and I thought we were just going for a drive or a chat. Instead, she took me to her friend's house. When we arrived, she introduced her friend, explaining that she had also lost her mum and was training to become a counsellor.

I looked at her. Then at Deby. Then back at her friend.

"Okay. So why are we here?"

Deby tried to explain gently: *"I just thought maybe she could speak to you—you know, help you process things."*

I was vicious. I looked at her friend and said, *"Excuse me. Are you bringing my mum back? Can you bring my mum back? No? Okay. Then what's the point? Please, let's go."*
And I walked out.

Deby followed, probably mortified. Her friend was left standing there—confused, maybe hurt. I didn't care. I was so consumed by my own pain that I couldn't see anyone else's.

Years later, I saw that friend again for the first time at Deby's dad's funeral this year. I went straight to her and apologised. I told her how sorry I was for being so rude, for dismissing her kindness, for throwing her attempt to help back in her face.

She was gracious. *"Listen, you don't have to apologise to me. I understand. I get it. Don't worry."*

But I did need to apologise—because even though grief explained my behaviour, it didn't excuse it.

That wasn't an isolated incident. There were others. Friends who tried to check in and I shut them out. People who offered support and I told them to leave me alone. Moments where I was so raw and angry that I lashed out at anyone who came too close.

My friends knew that wasn't me. They knew my real personality—kind, warm, thoughtful. But grief had turned me into someone unrecognisable, and even knowing that didn't erase the damage I caused.

When the fog lifted slightly, when I could finally see what I'd done, I started apologising. Some people accepted. Some didn't. Some were confused, wondering why I was apologising again after already doing so once before.

What they didn't understand was that grief comes in waves—and so does clarity about the harm it caused.

The first apology might have been surface level: something I said because I knew I should, not because I fully grasped the weight of what I'd done. The second apology came from a deeper place—the recognition that grief may explain your behaviour, but it can never excuse it.

Not everyone forgave me. And that's okay. Some people couldn't separate the grief from the person. Some decided they didn't want me in their lives anymore, and I had to respect that.

What mattered wasn't whether they accepted my apology. What mattered was that I owned my part—that I acknowledged how loving someone fiercely and losing them suddenly doesn't give you a free pass to hurt others without consequence.

Grief made me cruel. But growth made me accountable.

And in the end, that accountability taught me something essential: the people who stayed weren't the ones I never hurt—they were the ones who saw me at my worst and still believed I could become better.

Deby: The Love That Stayed

Everybody needs a Deby.

She is the friend who loves me in the way I love others, and that is rare beyond measure. Even when I was harsh, distant, or unkind, she never left. She stayed, she checked in, she pushed past my silences until I could no longer deny that I wasn't managing this alone.

Her love is soft, steady, and sister-like. She holds me with the kind of patience that feels like family: the kind of unwavering presence that doesn't flinch when you show your worst self. Her family has become mine. Her mum and sisters welcomed me into their home, giving me another place to belong when mine felt so painfully empty.

I wasn't always easy to love in grief. I was mean, cold, rude, angry. I snapped without warning or reason, withdrew without explanation, shut down when connection felt too dangerous—too much like another thing that could be taken away. Yet Deby never left. She kept checking in, not out of duty but out of pure devotion. Her love was persistent, steady, unshaken by my worst moments.

Now, as Deby grieves the loss of both her parents, I try to carry her the way she once carried me, reminding her that love does not abandon, and that even in the deepest emptiness, she is not alone.

Deby's love taught me that endurance is its own language—one that doesn't need to be loud to be loyal.

Everybody needs a Deby: the one who doesn't give up on you, even when you've given up on yourself.

Sometimes I worry that I'll never be able to show up for Deby the way she did for me. Not because I don't want to, but because adulthood complicates love. We are both older now, busier, carrying more than we used to. Showing up isn't as simple as knocking on a door or sitting beside each other until the storm passes. But even in that worry, I remind myself that love can evolve. It doesn't always look the same—sometimes it becomes quieter, slower, stretched across miles—yet still steady, still true.

"Even when you push love away, the right people will stay."

A Table for Deby

I wanted to show up for her the way she once showed up for me, even if it looked different now.

When Deby's dad died in 2025, only a few years after losing her mum, I realised the depth of the grief she now carried. To lose both parents—both anchors of her world—felt unimaginable. I thought about how she had once carried me through my own loss, how faithfully she had stayed when others drifted away, and I wondered how I could be that kind of presence for her.

The truth is, adulthood makes showing up harder. When we were younger, Deby could knock on my door, sit on my bed, and not leave until she was sure I was okay. Now life is crowded with work, children, and commitments: you can't just appear at someone's house the way you could at twenty-two. But I still wanted to find a way to show up.

So I created a group chat. At her dad's funeral, I reconnected with Tracy—one of our old friends from the circle we'd shared when we were younger—and one of Deby's close friends. Together, we began to build a small circle around her. I called it *A Table for Deby*—my way of making sure she would never sit alone.

Later, she changed the name to *Hot Girl Walks*—walking was what she loved most. Whilst I might prefer dinners or evenings of live music, Deby found peace in movement, and so we walked with her.

I'm glad she did. Choosing walks instead of my usual dinners or music nights gave me something new—something surprisingly healing. I've always loved the gym and running, but I'd never gone on walks with friends before. This felt different—slower, softer, almost meditative. It became its own kind of therapy: movement and conversation blending into something that quietly steadied us both.

The group became more than grief support. It became a space to talk about life: our happiness, our heaviness, our frustrations, our quiet hopes. A place where we could laugh as easily as we could cry; where healing happened mid-stride, under open skies, one conversation at a time.

Those walks also taught me something. Tracy, who hasn't yet lost anyone close, confessed she lives with anticipatory grief—fearing the day her parents will die, the day the weight of responsibility will fall on her shoulders as the strong one in her family. She opened up about an illness she carried silently when we were younger, when part of her face was paralysed and she spent months in hospital without many of us even knowing.

Hearing her speak reminded me of something important: pain is everywhere, even in those who still have their parents. Their grief is different, but no less real.

Creating that group chat showed me something simple yet profound. In building a table for Deby, I was also building one for myself—proof that love doesn't need to be carried alone. Sometimes it simply needs a place to walk beside you.

Love can be heavy, but when shared, it steadies. That is what the table—and the walks—became: a circle strong enough to hold us all.

Tare: The Steady Presence

"When life falls apart, he is the stillness that holds."

Tare has always been the quiet constant in my loudest seasons.

He is my favourite male cousin. Growing up, I was intimidated by him. He was a teaser—always mocking and bantering—and as a young person, I took it seriously. I thought he was strict, maybe even mean. But as I got older, I realised Tare was just Tare. You banter back, and suddenly you're laughing together instead of taking offence.

When I relocated to the UK, Tare was already living there. That's when we really bonded. He became like a brother to me, filling the space I craved from my actual brothers: the socialising, the hanging out, the adventures. Tare was the one who said yes when I wanted to go somewhere, do something spontaneous, just exist outside the heaviness of life.

He is intelligent, adventurous, and protective. He helped me proofread my university work when I was drowning in deadlines. We travelled together often—exploring new places, creating memories. He has always been the person I can call, the one who shows up without hesitation.

On 7 July, Tare was there from the start. When my world collapsed, he didn't try to fix me; he just stayed—steady, quiet, present. In that chaos, his stillness grounded me, a calm I could cling to when everything else felt impossible.

Years later, during the COVID lockdown, when isolation became unbearable and I reached my breaking point, I called Tare. "Please, I need to come stay with you." He didn't hesitate. I stayed with him for two months.

During that time at Tare's, I cried often—sometimes quietly, sometimes uncontrollably. I was still healing from the isolation of being by myself, which triggered missing my mum. The panic attacks, the anxiety, the fear—all of it overwhelmed me. He would look at me, concerned, probably wondering what he could do to help. But he never tried to fix me. He just let me cry. No judgement. No pressure to pull myself together. Just presence.

After those two months, I realised I couldn't live alone again. I needed a flatmate. And Tare drove me to every single house viewing. Every single one.

"Tare, can you take me to the airport?"

"Yes."

"Tare, can you help me with this?"

"Yes."

That's who Tare is—always saying yes when I need him, always showing up.

That's what he has always been: steady, present, the kind of person who doesn't need to say much because his actions speak everything. When life falls apart, he's the one who catches me. When I need space to grieve without performance, he gives it to me. When I'm ready to laugh again, he's already cracking jokes, waiting for me to banter back.

Tare remains in my life today—still my fun cousin, still my favourite male cousin. We still travel together, still create new memories. He reminds me that family isn't just blood. It's the people who show up when you call, who hold you when you fall, and who stand beside you without needing to understand everything you're going through.

Thank you, Tare, for always saying yes. For catching me when I fell. For being steady when everything else was chaos.

In every season of my life—grief, joy, laughter, chaos—Tare has been proof that love doesn't always speak; sometimes it simply stays.

Yasmina: The Seed Planter

In 2009, Yasmina introduced me to fitness and running. She would travel forty minutes just to lace up beside me and say, "Let's go." At the time, it felt like ordinary friendship. Sweaty runs, laughter between breaths, the kind of discipline that feels casual when you're young. Only years later did I realise she had planted the seed that would grow into my lifeline.

When my mum died, the gym became the place that saved me. It was where I poured rage into dumbbells, where sweat replaced words, where exhaustion numbed the ache that never left. And every time I walked into that space, I remembered who had given me the gift of movement in the first place: Yasmina.

She wasn't close by when my mum died. Life had pulled us apart, not through conflict but through distance. She didn't know how deeply the seed she planted would one day sustain me. For years I carried an unspoken gratitude. Thank you for saving me without even knowing it.

Eventually, we reconnected. Yasmina even sat with me on my podcast, where we spoke openly about loss and survival. By then, her own grief had found her: losing her mum, her cousin, and a stillborn baby. Grief reshaped her as it had reshaped me, and our friendship became a mirror of survival, reflecting both what we'd lost and what we'd found again in each other.

The runs in 2009 weren't just miles on pavements. They were seeds that would bloom into resilience, into refuge, into a rhythm that carried me through nights I thought I wouldn't survive.

Now, as she walks her own road of loss, I stand with her as she once unknowingly stood with me. Yasmina remains in my life today, and our bond is stronger for all we've both survived. What began as casual runs became proof that sometimes love is planted long before you realise you'll need its harvest.

"Sometimes a friend gifts you something years before you realise you will need it."

Joy: The Midnight Shelter

Joy is the first friend I made after relocating from Nigeria to the UK—the first person I confided in about my panic attacks, even before I had the language to name them properly.

She was the one I called in the middle of the night, shaking and certain I was going to die. At 3 AM, when panic had my heart racing and my chest locked tight, she opened her door, let me crawl into her bed, and simply stayed. My body did not calm, but I felt safe. Safe in the only way that mattered: if death did come, at least I would not be alone.

She was the first friend I trusted enough to say, "*Something is happening to me, and I don't know what it is.*" Her response was simple but life-altering: "*Go to the GP.*" That became the beginning of naming my panic instead of drowning in it.

Joy's love was a practical shelter. She didn't erase the fear, but she refused to let me face it in isolation. And it wasn't just her. Her mum worried for me too, saying: *"Make sure you open the door for her. Stay awake until she's safely inside."* Her family welcomed me like their own, covering me in the places I could not cover myself. Joy has this quiet, calming way about her—gentle, steady, and soft-spoken. Even in my panic, her presence felt like stillness. She never made me feel like a burden, not even in my most fragile moments.

Now, as Joy grieves her own mother, I do my best to shelter her in return. Not in the exact way she once held me, but with the same tenderness—proof that the circle of love can continue, even in loss. Watching her now, I see my former self—fragile, unravelled, learning to breathe through unbearable pain. I wish I could take her sorrow away, but I know I can't. So I stay close, sometimes in silence, sometimes in words, doing what she once did for me: simply being there.

Joy remains in my life, still opening doors, still being the kind of friend who makes safety feel possible.

It's a rare gift to have a Joy—the friend who opens the door and keeps it open.

"Safety isn't always calm. Sometimes it is simply knowing someone will open the door."

Tawa: The Grounded Anchor

Tawa is more than a family friend. She became my anchor when I was drowning, almost like a personal counsellor in those years when everything felt like it was spinning out of control.

She didn't just comfort me. She equipped me. She helped me see patterns when everything felt like chaos, offered me structure when I had none, and reminded me I wasn't collapsing: I was grieving, and there's a difference worth understanding.

Her love was constructive, never performative. She didn't try to replace my mum or silence my pain. Instead, she gave me language when I had none, perspective when I was blind to my own survival, tools when my hands felt completely empty.

Tawa never cried with me. She didn't offer soft words or gentle embraces. She wasn't emotional in the way I was, and at first, that felt jarring. But that steadiness, that complete lack of emotional mirroring, was exactly what I needed. Where I was falling apart, she remained whole. Where I was drowning in feeling, she stayed grounded in clarity.

She knew I couldn't be by myself. Fear of being alone was one of the symptoms I experienced in grief, one of the ways loss manifested in my body and mind. So she brought me along to work, offering presence and routine when solitude felt dangerous. She created structure when my days felt formless. She asked the right questions, not to fix me, but to help me understand myself. Her steadiness kept me from sinking entirely.

Some friends hold you by crying with you. Tawa held me by refusing to fall apart alongside me. Both are love. Both matter. And I needed both.

Tawa remains in my life today, still grounding me, still offering wisdom when I need it most. Her guidance stays with me in ways I can't always name, but always feel.

"The right people don't just comfort you. They give you tools to stand when you cannot."

Jenny: The Soft Sister

Jenny, my cousin, is still my softness.

Jenny was the one I called on 7 July. When panic had me trembling, she answered. She didn't hesitate—she came straight to me.

In the hours when everything fell apart, she caught me when I fell and held me upright when my body gave way. She didn't try to fix it or fill the silence. She absorbed it—the shaking, the sobbing, the wordless grief. She simply stayed—steady, calm, present.

Her stillness steadied me when I was lost in chaos, keeping me tethered to life when I wanted to let go. In that moment, love looked like silence and soft hands holding me up when I couldn't hold myself.

Where Tawa gave me structure, Jenny gives me permission to surrender.

She cried with me when I had no words, sat in silence when I had no strength, and let me collapse without a trace of judgement. She held space for the ugly, desperate parts of grief that I was too ashamed to show anyone else.

She is my family, but she is also my friend—loyal, gentle, and unwavering, the kind of presence that doesn't need to fix me to make me feel safe. When I couldn't speak, she sat quietly. When I sobbed until I was breathless, she handed me tissues and stayed close.

There were times I worried Jenny might think I didn't value her way of loving me. That because I sometimes sought Tawa's practical wisdom, I didn't need her emotional tenderness. But that was never true. The truth is, I needed both. There were days when Tawa's grounded clarity saved me from drowning. And there were other days when only Jenny's tears, her willingness to feel my pain alongside me, could reach the parts of me that were too broken for words.

Her emotional strength isn't weakness. It's courage. To sit in someone else's pain without trying to fix it, to cry with them without needing them to stop crying, to hold space for the mess without tidying it up takes a kind of bravery that not everyone has. Jenny has that bravery. She always has.

Jenny's loyalty to me was fierce and absolute. She sometimes hung out with me and my friends, and witnessed some of my worst moments during grief: the lashing out, the meanness, the rudeness that wasn't really me. Jenny knew this wasn't who I was. But she stood beside me without question, loyal to me in everything, never blaming or pointing fingers.

That kind of loyalty is rare. She would have gently told me when I crossed a line, but instead, her loyalty was unshakeable. She knew this was a passing phase, a symptom of grief rather than who I truly was. Because of that, she didn't feel the need to call me out or correct me. If something had truly crossed into harmful or dangerous territory (which it didn't), she would have spoken to me quietly, just between us. But for everything else, she simply stood by me without judgement, choosing me fiercely and completely, even at my worst.

Sometimes grief needs anchors to hold you up. Other times it needs someone willing to sink down beside you.

Jenny is that: the tender reminder that love doesn't demand performance, that I don't need to wear strength like a costume to still be worthy of care and attention. She remains that softness for me today, still holding space, still reminding me that I am loved exactly as I am.

"Softness is also strength. To be held in tears is to remember you are still loved."

Tobenna: The Constant Flame

From twenty-two, when I lost my mum, until twenty-seven, I drifted. Birthdays came and went unnoticed, unacknowledged, uncelebrated. I refused to acknowledge time, as if denying birthdays could somehow deny her absence. I lived on autopilot.

Existing, but not truly alive.

Then came Tobenna. My flatmate in Nigeria, stubborn in her love, relentless in her care. She refused to let me disappear, no matter how many calls I ignored or how many times I begged her not to message me. She kept showing up, knocking at the edges of my silence until I had no choice but to feel seen.

On my twenty-seventh birthday, she tricked me. She told me I was meeting a Greek guy for a blind date. I got dressed, laughing in the car with her as music blasted, believing every single word of her elaborate story. But when we arrived at Crossroads Bar in Lagos, I walked into a room full of friends shouting, "Surprise!"

It was my first birthday dinner in seven years. I cried that night, not only for the love in the room, but for the shocking realisation of time itself: I was twenty-seven. Six entire years had vanished whilst I wasn't looking, slipping away like water through my fingers.

That night, Tobenna gave me back my years. She reminded me that even when grief steals presence, the right people will pull you back into life.

Tobenna remains a force in my life today, still refusing to let me disappear, still showing up with that same relentless love. She is proof that some friendships don't just survive grief; they become stronger because of it.

"Even if grief makes you disappear, the right people will find ways to call you back."

Seun: The Courage Keeper

"Some friends give you courage you didn't know you had"

When my mum died, I refused to see her body.

At the hospital, after the doctor told me she was gone, a nurse came to ask quietly if I wanted to see her one last time before they took her away.

Every part of me screamed no. I couldn't bear the thought of seeing her lifeless, of that image replacing every living memory I had of her. I wanted to remember her alive—laughing, teasing me through my bedroom door, calling my name in the mornings.

But Seun didn't let me run from it.

Her presence had already pulled me back from the edge outside the hospital, where I'd been contemplating running into traffic. Now she stood beside me in the corridor, steady and calm, whilst I trembled with fear.

Her voice was soft but unshakable, a quiet strength that met my resistance. She told me I might regret it if I didn't go in, that even though it felt impossible now, it could become a moment I would hold on to later. When I still shook my head, she said simply, "I'll come with you."

Because of her courage, I finally walked into that room.

She walked in beside me, holding my hand as I looked at my mum's face for the last time. Even in death, her face was still soft, still hers—not yet touched by the decay that would come later. In that moment, Seun gave me something I could never have done for myself: the chance to say goodbye whilst my mum still looked like my mum.

That image—the one Seun helped me face—became the one I chose to hold closest.

Years later, when another memory tried to overwrite it—a version of my mum I couldn't bear—I still held on to the gentler image: her face at the hospital, still soft, still peaceful.

Even though life has taken us down different paths, I'll always be grateful for that day—for the calm she gave me without even realising it.

Some friends don't just stand beside you; they gift you the courage to face goodbye and a memory gentle enough to last a lifetime.

Sometimes one quiet act of love becomes the thread that leads you back to yourself—long after the moment has passed.

Chizee: The Relentless Knock

When I fled London for Nigeria, I told myself distance would protect me.

The UK carried too many reminders of my mum, but in Nigeria her presence felt faint, almost absent. I convinced myself that living where her shadow didn't follow would make the grief easier to bear.

That's when I met Chizee. Steadfast, relentless, and tender all at once.

We bonded through running and gym sessions. Sweating, pushing each other, laughing between sets. She became my companion in both discipline and distraction, the friend who matched my pace when I ran forward and waited patiently when I fell behind.

Every time I disappeared after a night of laughter or a day of workouts, she knocked gently on my door.

Inside, I stayed hidden, sobbing louder with every knock, unable to explain the storm tearing through me. But she never judged, never demanded answers. She showed care through action. Persistence instead of pressure, presence instead of pity.

"Hello? I don't know if you're in there... just checking in, making sure you're okay. I haven't heard from you, I'm worried about you."

She would drive to me, call, and knock again, never knowing if I was inside, but still refusing to let my silence win. Her persistence was love. Steady, unshaken, always reaching for me through the door.

Her knocks became proof. Someone saw me, someone cared, even when I couldn't respond. Even when I chose distance, she remained.

She built belonging where I only expected isolation, making me feel at home, loved, and held even when words failed me completely.

Looking back, I owe her both gratitude and apology.

Thank you, Chizee, for never leaving. For being proof that love can be steady without words. And I'm sorry for the times I pushed you away, too lost in my storm to let you in.

Chizee remains in my life today, still steady, still present, still reminding me that love doesn't give up.

"Sometimes the gentlest knock becomes the loudest reminder: you are not alone."

Shamim: The Teacher of Gentle Check-Ins

Shamim taught me one of the greatest lessons: how to check in without demand. I was oceans away in Nigeria, yet her words cut across distance like steady signals in the dark.

Her messages were always simple and soft. "Thinking of you." "I love you." "No need to reply." She never punished my silence. She never pushed for answers. She reminded me that love does not need proof, only presence.

What shook me most was her timing. Her messages always landed on the exact days I was breaking down indoors—crying, isolating, convinced no one noticed my absence from the world. And then her words would appear on my phone screen. I would sob even harder, not from despair but from the reminder that someone still cared.

She showed me that sometimes the most powerful support is the gentlest touch. Love that does not press, demand, or intrude, but still refuses to let you feel forgotten.

Over time, I found myself doing the same—sending quiet check-ins, simple messages, soft reminders. It became the way I learned to love back: gently, patiently, without expectation.

Shamim continues to check in, still teaching me the power of gentle love, still reminding me that presence doesn't require perfection.

"The gentlest words can become the strongest lifeline: no reply needed, only presence."

Lessons in Loss and Loyalty

Grief changes who stays at your table. Some vanish without explanation. Some surprise you with their steadiness. Some step closer than they've ever been. And some walk with you only for a season, yet leave treasures you would never have had without them.

Every friend mentioned here (Esse, Deby, Tare, Yasmina, Joy, Tawa, Jenny, Tobenna, Seun, Chizee, and Shamim) gave me something different. None of them gave me everything. But together, they helped me survive.

That is the truth of grief and friendship: no one person can carry you. Piece by piece, love gathers. And even in silence, you are not alone.

To my newer friends, the ones who entered my life years later: thank you. Thank you for holding me in these recent seasons, for allowing me to retreat when I needed distance, for still checking in when I go quiet, and for not mistaking my silences as rejection. Even now, in 2025, when I isolate or ignore messages, you remind me I am not forgotten. Your presence continues the story of survival—living proof that love keeps finding its way back to me.

"Some friends carry you through the first storm. Others arrive years later. Together, they prove that love keeps finding you, again and again."

A Note to All Who Grieve Friendship

If you're reading this and you've lost friends, or if you've been the friend who didn't know how to show up, know this: grief exposes our humanity, our limits, our fears. Some friendships cannot survive the weight. Others become stronger for carrying it together.

If you've felt alone in your grief, if you've wondered why people disappeared or why their love felt insufficient, remember that different people love in different languages. The friend who checks in weekly may be showing as much love as the friend who sits with you in silence.

And if you're the friend trying to support someone in grief: your imperfect presence matters more than your perfect absence. Show up, even when you don't know what to say. Stay, even when it's uncomfortable. Your consistency will be remembered long after your words are forgotten.

How Grief Redefined Friendship

Navigating friendship through grief taught me lessons I never wanted to learn. Some came slowly, over years. Others arrived suddenly, in moments of clarity that changed everything. Here's what I know now:

Saying when I was struggling helped—even if it was just letting someone know I might go quiet for a while.

Being clear about what I needed—space, company, or silence—made things easier for both of us.

Offering my loved ones language helped bridge the gap. I shared words that comforted me, or gently explained what felt too heavy.

Setting boundaries with love kept friendships alive. Teaching friends how to support me created space for connection.

Noticing who showed up without being asked mattered. Consistency meant more than perfect words.

Releasing those who left with grace protected my peace. I honoured what they gave, but saved my energy for those who remained.

Making space for new friendships with people who understood grief opened unexpected doors.

Honouring the friendships that faded felt important. They mattered, even if they couldn't last.

Writing the apology when my heart nudged me served everyone. Healing benefited me as much as them.

For You, If Friendship Feels Fragile

Who did you expect to be there, and how did their response shape your understanding of friendship?

Which friendship faded during grief, and what did that teach you about love's limitations?

Who surprised you by staying, and how can you thank them?

Which new friendship has been an anchor you didn't expect?

Looking back, can you spot one small act of love you missed at the time?

The Gathering of Love

"Friendship after loss is not the same as friendship before. It's tested, refined, and sometimes reduced to its essence. What remains is often stronger, truer, and more precious than what you had before."

Chapter Seven

The Changing Shapes of Love

"Grief doesn't erase love; it reshapes it into forms you never expected."

When loss arrives, love doesn't end—it just changes shape, the way water becomes ice or steam. It's still the same substance, only transformed by forces beyond your control.

At first, grief feels like an open wound: raw, consuming, impossible to live beside. You can't imagine the pain softening, can't imagine a day when you'll feel anything but absence. Slowly, almost imperceptibly, the wound becomes a scar. Not because the love is smaller, but because it has learned new ways to live inside you.

After my mum died, love shifted in every corner of my life like a house resettling after an earthquake. It reshaped how I loved myself, how I loved others, and how I could receive love in return. The transformation was subtle at first, then undeniable.

Some days I felt completely shut off, untouchable, unable to accept affection because grief had filled all my available space. My heart was occupied territory, with grief as the tenant who left no room for visitors.

Other days I craved closeness so intensely, that I clung to people too tightly. I read silence into every pause, abandonment into every delay. I analysed text messages, replayed cancelled plans, panicked at the slightest sign of distance. The fear of losing again made me desperate in ways that probably pushed people away: the very thing I dreaded most.

Grief doesn't just reshape pain; it reshapes capacity. It makes you notice the friends who steady you without being asked, and the ones who quietly disappear when the weight grows heavy. It sharpens gratitude for the smallest gestures: a meal left at your door, a call that comes at exactly the right moment, a hand on your back when words feel impossible.

Love after loss is heavier, sharper, and more urgent. You say "I love you" more often because you know how quickly last words can become final ones. You hug longer because you remember the shock of arms gone forever. You notice more. You linger more. You hold on with the knowledge that nothing is promised.

But this reshaping isn't always gentle. Sometimes love feels jagged and unpredictable. One day you're overflowing with it; the next day you feel hollow, unable to accept even the simplest kindness. You pull away from the people who care. You cling to connections that aren't healthy. You live in extremes, because the middle ground has been stolen.

Dating After Loss

"How do you let someone see you when your heart still belongs to the past?"

Dating became another place where grief exposed me. Raw and broken, every attempt at connection felt like navigating a minefield blindfolded.

How do you explain the absence that defines you to a stranger? How do you laugh over drinks when you know you might fall apart in the taxi home? How do you sit across from someone new when part of you is convinced that letting anyone in is just inviting more loss?

There was a man I went on a few dates with. He was kind, easy to talk to, the sort of person I should have been able to open up to. But I wasn't there. My body was sitting at the table, smiling politely, but my mind was elsewhere: in the silence of my bedroom, in the memory of the hospital corridor, in the echo of my mum's last breath.

He noticed. He tilted his head as if to ask silently, *Where are you?* But I couldn't explain. At that time, even saying "my mum died" felt impossible. The words caught in my throat like a betrayal, as though admitting her absence made it more final.

So I stayed quiet. He was left with a version of me that was distracted, absent, unreachable. And then, of course, it faded away.

That became the pattern. Not with him specifically, but with anyone who got too close. I would go on dates, laugh at the right moments, answer questions about my job or my hobbies. But the second someone leaned in (emotionally, not physically) I vanished. A slow fade, a cancelled plan, a text left on read.

It wasn't cruelty. It was self-protection. If I never let anyone close enough to matter, they could never die and destroy me the way losing my mum had. The logic was airtight. The loneliness was unbearable.

It took years to understand that I wasn't protecting myself from future loss. I was punishing myself for surviving. Every connection I sabotaged was me proving I didn't deserve to be loved when she was gone.

Years later, when I launched my podcast, he reappeared. Out of nowhere, a message lit up my phone screen:

"I've been keeping tabs on your channel and videos. I'm immensely proud of you and what you're doing. People lose their parents early and don't know how to navigate life or grief. Your platform is needed. Keep it up."

I sat with that message for a long time. Here was someone who had once seen me drowning silently, someone I couldn't let in, and now he was affirming the very thing that silence had grown into.

That's the strange circle of love after loss. Sometimes what you couldn't say in the moment becomes the very thing you are eventually known for. And sometimes the people who saw you at your most broken become witnesses to your becoming whole.

The Shape of Self-Love

Grief didn't just change how I dated. It changed how I saw myself.

There were months I withdrew completely, convinced that moving forward meant leaving her behind. I couldn't allow myself happiness without immediately acknowledging her absence.

But slowly, I began to understand that self-love after grief is not indulgence. It's survival.

It took nine years before I could say "I'm happy" without feeling like I was betraying her. Even now, I have to dilute it: "I'm happy, but I'd be happier if my mum was here." I need to acknowledge her absence alongside my joy, as if happiness without mentioning her means I've forgotten. I haven't. I never will.

Self-love became one of grief's strangest new shapes. Not roses and candles. Just breath, food, shower, bed. The basics. Choosing to keep going when stopping felt easier.

When Love Learned to Breathe Again

Love after loss is not the same as love before. It bends, it shifts, it reshapes, but it doesn't vanish. It continues, finding new forms to live in—in memory, in ritual, in tenderness, in how fiercely you hold the people who remain.

Love after grief is not naive. It is scarred, cautious, often trembling. But it is also the purest kind of love: the kind that knows how fragile life is and chooses to show up anyway.

Grief makes you love differently—slower, deeper, and with clearer eyes. It teaches you to recognise what is real and to stop chasing what isn't. Losing my mum taught me that love should never need convincing. If it isn't pure, honest, and organic, I let it go. I no longer cling to what drains me or fight for what doesn't flow naturally. Life is too short to hold on to anything that isn't true.

And maybe that's the truest kind of love—one that learns to live in every form it's given.

For You, If Love Feels Impossible Now

What has love taught you since loss?

Have you noticed how your capacity to give or receive love has changed?

How do you protect your heart now—and how do you let it soften again?

In what ways has grief deepened the way you love yourself or others?

Reshaped Love

"Love doesn't die. It adapts. It reshapes itself around the absence, and in that reshaping, it keeps on living."

Chapter Eight

The Loneliness Lie

"Loneliness in grief lies, but it feels true."

Loneliness is one of grief's sharpest weapons. It whispers lies that feel like truth: that you are unseen, that if you vanished no one would notice, that you exist in a bubble of pain no one can reach.

For me, that isolation came from losing the one person who checked on me every single day. My mum was my anchor, the voice that asked how I was and waited for the real answer. Friends cared. Family cared. But no one could replace her daily presence, her intuitive knowing, the way she read my mood from my voice. Without that, silence pressed in so hard I sometimes believed I could disappear and it would take a while before anyone noticed.

This is grief's lie. It magnifies absence until it drowns out everything else. It feels true because what you lost was unique. But unique does not mean unloved. It just means learning to recognise love in new, unfamiliar forms.

Loneliness cuts deepest in ordinary moments. When you reach for your phone to share a joke, when you have good news and the one who'd have been most excited isn't there, when you're sick and the one who'd have fussed over you is gone. It's not only missing them. It's feeling invisible in a world that carries on whilst you're still standing in ruins.

And then comes another lie: that asking for help makes you a burden.

The Silence That Spoke for Me

"Sometimes not calling is how grief keeps you safe."

People say 'reach out if you need help.' But what do you say when everyone already knows the problem? My friends knew I'd lost my mum. There was nothing new to report. No crisis to announce. Just ongoing, relentless absence.

So I didn't call. Not because I didn't want support, but because I couldn't explain what I needed. How do you ask for help with something that can't be fixed?

The only time I reached out was when grief showed up physically—the panic attacks that sent me to Joy's door at 3 AM. Those I could name. But the quiet, crushing loneliness? That stayed silent.

Once, I called Esse in the middle of the night, too scared to sleep. "You have to stay on the phone with me," I said. And she did—quietly, patiently, until we both drifted off.

That's the thing about grief: it doesn't always need grand gestures. Sometimes, it just needs someone to stay on the line while the night passes.

When I Go Silent

"Silence isn't absence; it's survival."

I'm still learning. When I'm low, I go quiet. I stay indoors, stay in bed, binge series, cry. Series save me. The gym helps. Music helps. Writing down my thoughts and feelings in my iPhone notes helps too. Writing this book helps. SayItKit gives me a thread of purpose. Journalling is new—not yet a habit, but a small way of finding myself again.

I don't keep an Anchors List anymore. Grief taught me not to place heavy expectations on people. But I do set gentle boundaries.

I created a soft script I send to friends when I go quiet:

"Hey honeys, I'm not in a happy, fun mood right now. I'm a bit down and quiet. I'm okay. If you don't hear from me, don't worry. If it's really important, please message me and I'll answer. Please, no personal questions or 'how are you feeling' right now. It's just one of my low episodes—a down time. I'm not up for deep chats, but I truly appreciate you holding me in your thoughts."

During episodes, I don't pick up calls. I usually explain afterwards, sometimes even laugh or cry with distance.

In my first year of grief, when panic attacks hit at night, I'd text Joy: "Are you home? I can't sleep. Can I come over?" She always said yes. No speeches, just an open door. That was then. Thirteen years on, I rarely reach out mid-episode. I retreat, and I speak once it passes.

Shamim understands my quiet, never takes it personally. Most friends respect it. Tobenna still pushes for calls. That's her nature. I try not to take it as pressure.

I move through the year in episodes. When one lands, I retreat. I'm practising saying no without guilt, and telling the truth in small ways. Sometimes asking isn't "help me." It's "please give me space." Both count.

The Lie Loneliness Told Me

"The lie is loud, but love is louder."

Loneliness feels absolute, but it isn't. The lie is loud, but love is present. Sometimes softer, sometimes different, but always there.

Noticing proof of care I'd overlooked helped. A friend texting at the exact moment I needed it. Someone remembering an anniversary without being reminded. Small acts that said: you matter.

On my hardest days, one small action made me feel a little less invisible. Watching a series, going for a short run or walk, or playing a song that reminded me of her—anything that proved I wasn't alone, even when loneliness roared otherwise.

I don't reach out as I used to, but I've learned something gentler: I'm not alone. I know that if I really needed to call someone, there are two or three people who would answer. Just knowing that is enough.

Anchoring my week with one small connection helped: a quick chat with my flatmate before retreating back to my room, a few minutes of being heard before I pressed play on another episode. Those small rhythms kept me tethered when isolation tempted me to disappear.

Most importantly, this truth: my worth was never measured by daily check-ins. My mum's presence was unique. Her absence does not mean I am unloved.

For You, If You Feel Invisible

What makes loneliness feel most unbearable for you? Is it silence, absence of routine contact, or something else?

Who could be your "Joy," the person you could reach out to at 3 AM if you needed?

What small ritual could remind you weekly that you're not invisible?

Always There

"You are not invisible. Loneliness can roar, but it does not tell the whole truth. Love is present, sometimes softer, sometimes different, but always there. I know this because on my worst nights, when I was convinced no one would notice if I disappeared, someone always texted. Not because they knew I was drowning, but because love has a way of showing up, even when you're too proud to ask for it."

Chapter Nine

Different Grief, Same House

"Even in the same home, grief speaks different languages to different hearts."

We are three siblings. Timi is the eldest, Tony is the middle child, and I am the youngest. The only daughter among two sons.

When my mum died, that birth order and gender difference shaped how we each carried the grief, and how we related to each other in the aftermath.

My mum was everything to me. Not just my mother, but my father, my sister, my brother, my protector, my god. She filled every role that mattered, answered every question, solved every problem. If I needed money, it was my mum. If I needed advice, emotional support, or simply someone who understood me completely, it was always her.

She was so present, so powerful, that I never really needed my brothers, Timi and Tony, for anything substantial. Not in a negative way, but because my mum was so all-encompassing she became my entire support system.

We are close, my brothers and I, but I didn't lean on them the way siblings often do. My mum was my everything, and they were simply my brothers.

When she died, nothing changed between us, except suddenly, I had no anchor. The two people closest to me, the ones who had lost the same person on the same devastating day, felt unreachable.

At twenty-two, I didn't have the language for what was happening. I was living in a bubble before loss hit: protected, naive, unaware of how depression or trauma worked. And so I was left by myself, drowning in experiences I couldn't name, carrying a weight I couldn't share.

I moved to Nigeria partly to escape my mum's presence, which haunted every street in London. But also because I thought distance might soften the grief. It didn't. Grief crossed oceans with me, and now I was facing it in isolation, far from the only people who knew her like I did.

My brothers don't know about the panic attacks that nearly drove me mad. They don't know about the sleepless nights when I was convinced I was dying, or the hallucinations where I saw her in crowds. They don't know about the nights I sat with gate men in Lagos because I couldn't bear the silence, or the long hours I spent circling the city in Ubers just to avoid being alone.

They know I miss our mum. They know I created a podcast about grief. But we've never spoken in detail about her death, never shared our darkest hours, never compared how we've survived the past thirteen years without her.

The irony is cruel. I spent nine episodes of my podcast listening to other people's grief stories, invited a counsellor and a psychotherapist to help them process pain. But when it came time for the final episode—the one where my brothers and I would finally speak about losing our mum—I couldn't do it.

We didn't even make it past the first question: "How did you find out our mum had died?" The moment the words left my lips, I broke down so badly the psychotherapist had to stop the session. The weight of sharing my pain, whilst hearing theirs, was too much to bear.

Timi: My Mum's Reflection

"He carries her tenderness, even when it costs him."

Timi reminds me of my mum. He mirrors her strength, her sense of responsibility, her way of putting children first no matter the cost. Just as she carried the weight of being both mother and father to us, I see Timi carrying that same weight for his own children. He doesn't measure love by roles or rules. He just gives it.

Watching him with his kids (the school runs, the quiet rhythms of bedtime) I see echoes of the way Mum poured herself into us. He puts them first in every possible way, sometimes to the point of forgetting himself. I admire it, even when I worry about the cost.

He wakes them, dresses them, takes them to school, shows up for every bedtime story and every meal, every homework check. He carries almost all of the load, whilst still holding down work and life. It is relentless, and yet he shows up with the same steady devotion that defined our mum.

It's why I often think of him as the best dad I know. Not because it's effortless, but because I know it isn't. He is stretched thin, but he gives everything anyway. And in that sacrifice, I see my mum alive again.

Sometimes I look at him and think, if Mum were here, she would have made this easier. She would have scooped those children up, given him space to breathe. No one else can do that like a mother.

We once spoke quietly about how grief had changed him. His girlfriend at the time had told me he was less affectionate, less communicative, harder than he used to be. I mentioned it to him gently. He nodded, sat in silence for a while, then finally said:

"Everything else feels minor now. When the one person who poured love into you every day is gone, you don't have much left to give."

I didn't push. His silence said enough.

Timi's grief speaks in resilience. In carrying on. In loving his children fiercely, even when he feels emptied himself.

Tony: My Mum's Fire

"His love burns differently, but it's love all the same."

Tony has always been harder for me to read. Where Timi carries my mum's openness and tenderness, Tony holds her fire—fierce and unyielding. He is more traditional in his ways, shaped by an older way of seeing the world. He believes certain roles belong to women, certain responsibilities to men.

As children, our sibling fights never felt equal to me. What he might have seen as ordinary squabbles, I experienced as being overpowered. Even now, we remember those moments differently: me insisting it was painful, him insisting I exaggerated. The truth probably sits somewhere between how it felt for me and how it looked to him.

Years later, the difference in how we see things hasn't gone away. One evening, whilst driving me home after a family gathering, we ended up circling back to those old memories. The car grew tense, old wounds crackled to the surface.

"You don't forget easily. Even with Mum, you still haven't let go. Your podcast just shows you can't move on."

And then his words broke me: *Move on.*

Two words that feel like knives when you're grieving.

I screamed: "How dare you. Forget my mum? Impossible. You don't tell someone to move on from their mother. You don't tell someone to forget the person who gave them life."

Never tell the grieving to get over it. Grief doesn't vanish. It reshapes. It softens, it flares, it lingers—but it never disappears.

Those words cut too deep, but underneath his bluntness, I know he wasn't trying to be cruel. He saw me struggling and wanted me free from the weight. His language of love just sounded like dismissal. My language of grief demanded acknowledgement.

And that's the lesson I keep learning—we love the same woman, but we grieve in different dialects. I think his way is to close the door, to keep moving forward, to fight through. My way is to keep her alive in memory: in words, in my podcast, in every breath.

Neither is wrong. Grief just speaks in many tongues, and when those languages collide, they wound. But even in the clash, love remains—reshaped, imperfect, still alive.

The Sister I Never Had

"Some griefs are doubled—the one you lost, and the one that never existed."

My brothers have each other.

They go for drinks. They call each other up. They share that brotherly bond that doesn't require explanation or performance. When one texts, the other responds. When life gets heavy, they know they can reach out to each other without it feeling strange or forced.

I watch from the outside, and the jealousy cuts deeper than I know how to explain.

It's not that I don't see my brothers. I do. We spend time

together, often with my nieces, at their houses or mine. We celebrate Christmas, share meals, show up for family moments. We're not distant. We're not estranged.

But there's a difference between family gatherings and the casual, spontaneous connection they share with each other. Going out for drinks just because. Hanging out without it being planned weeks in advance. The ease of picking up the phone and saying "let's meet up" without it feeling formal or forced.

That's what they have with each other. And that's what I don't have with them.

It's not that I don't love my brothers. I do. But they have something I will never have: each other. A sibling who understands their specific experience, who shares their exact loss, who doesn't need translation to understand what this grief feels like for them.

I am the only daughter. The only sister. And in grief, that loneliness feels unbearable.

If I had a sister, I think everything would be lighter. Not easier, because grief is never easy, but lighter. Someone to cry with at 2 AM without feeling like I'm burdening her. Someone who would understand the specific ache of losing your mother as a daughter, not as a son. Someone who might check in on me the way my brothers check in on each other. Someone who could sit beside me in silence, sharing the quiet grief and memories that words cannot hold, holding space for the heaviness without needing explanation.

When I try to create that connection with my brothers, suggesting we go for dinners, drinks or try to spend time together the way they do with each other, it never quite happens. Not because they're cruel. Not because they don't care. But because we grieve in different languages, and I am speaking one they don't fully understand.

Now they have their children too. Timi has his daughters and his newborn son. Tony has his daughter. And sometimes they spend time together: brothers bonding, cousins playing, families merging in ways that feel natural for them.

I hear about it secondhand. My nieces mention it casually: "Oh yeah, I saw Maya this weekend." And my heart sinks. Why didn't they call me? Why didn't they invite me?

It's not that I expect an invitation to everything. But the pattern stings. They have each other, they have their children connecting them even more deeply, and I am the one left on the outside looking in.

I don't know what they talk about when they're together. Maybe they don't talk about Mum at all. Maybe they do, but in ways I wouldn't recognise. Maybe they're just as lost as I am, but at least they're lost together.

I'm lost alone.

That's the jealousy no one talks about in sibling grief: not just missing the person you lost, but missing the sibling you never had. The one who would have held this weight with you in the exact way you needed.

I will never have a sister. That loss sits alongside my mother's absence, quieter but just as permanent. And some days, that loneliness feels like its own kind of grief.

The Different Languages of Love

"We may love the same person, but we never grieve them in the same way."

This is how grief works in families. Some process it together, making it a shared project. Others carry it privately, assuming that loving the same person means grieving them in the same way.

But grief is as individual as love itself. We may have lost the same woman, but each of us lost a different relationship. Timi lost his confidante. Tony lost his anchor. I lost my everything.

For now, we love each other from different rooms. We grieve separately, honour her individually. Maybe that will change. Maybe it won't. But the love is still there, even in the silence.

Still, I hope someday we'll try again—to sit together, to speak her name, to remember her not in fragments but as a whole. Maybe one day we'll record that conversation on my podcast, or maybe we'll just have it quietly—in a shared space, without microphones or cameras—a quiet moment to meet in our loss, to bridge the silence, to see that even through distance, love remains. Just the three of us, remembering the woman who made us who we are.

I used to think love spoke one language—constant, clear, universal. But grief showed me it's a collection of dialects, each shaped by how we survive. Sometimes we shout. Sometimes we whisper. Sometimes silence is the only translation we have left. What matters is that the love is still there, even if it arrives in an unfamiliar tongue.

When Love Needs Translation

Everyone grieves differently, even when they've lost the same person. My grief is valid even if it doesn't look like theirs.

Assuming others are coping better because they look stronger is misleading. Grief wears many faces.

Offering gentle invitations, not demands, opens doors. Saying "I'm struggling today" may create space that "We need to talk about Mum" would close.

Making space for different grief styles matters: some need words, others need silence. Both deserve respect.

Timing matters. The conversation impossible today may become healing years from now.

For You, If Your Family Doesn't Understand

When you look at how each person grieves, what differences hurt you the most—and which remind you that love can take many forms?

Have you ever mistaken someone's silence for not caring? What might their quiet actually be saying?

What language does your grief speak—action, withdrawal, anger, prayer, laughter?

If your family could understand one thing about your pain, what would you want them to know?

The Common Thread

"Grief may speak different languages to different hearts, but love remains the common thread. And if love is the root, then even silence can still mean we are bound together."

Chapter Ten

When God Went Silent

Trigger Warning: This chapter speaks openly about faith, loss, and the crisis of belief that followed my mother's death. It may be painful for readers who are grieving or questioning their own faith. Please read gently, and only as you feel able.

"When the divine feels absent, you must decide what remains worthy of your faith."

On 7 July, as I stood outside the bathroom listening to my mum's laboured breathing, I prayed harder than I had ever prayed in my life.

I was raised Christian, taught that God answers prayers, faith can move mountains, and healing comes if you call earnestly enough. My whole understanding of prayer was simple: God responds when you really need Him. Good things happen to faithful people. Prayer works.

But until that day, I had never truly tested this belief. Life had been kind to me. I hadn't faced hardship that demanded divine intervention. My prayers were routine—daily words of gratitude for health, family, and life. They were maintenance prayers, not desperate pleas.

This was different. This was the first time I asked God for something urgent, something beyond my control.

God, please help my mum. My mum shall not die. She shall live. Lord, please help my mum. Please help my mum.

I repeated the words like a mantra—a contract I was trying to enforce. I knew what I was seeing was bad, terrifying even, and prayer felt like the only tool left to fight against the inevitable.

The ambulance came. They took her to the hospital. And then, minutes or hours later—time had dissolved—someone told me she had died.

And in that moment, something in me died too. Not only my mum, but my faith.

The God I had been taught about crumbled instantly. If He answers prayers, why not mine? If He loves His children, *why let my mum die despite my desperate pleas?*

Two weeks later, Tawa and Jenny took me to church. I was raw, fragile, still reeling. When the pastor asked if anyone needed prayer, they nudged me forward. I stood before the congregation, surrounded by believers convinced that God could heal what was broken.

But inside me, a bitter thought formed: Why am I here? This God didn't answer me when I needed Him most. He let my mum die. What could I possibly ask Him for now?

I left that service feeling more disconnected from faith than ever. Rituals felt hollow. Promises felt false. The community felt like they were speaking a language I no longer understood.

I stopped believing in God that day. It wasn't gradual. It was immediate and absolute—a door slamming shut on everything I'd been taught about divine love and protection.

In time, I realised it wasn't God I was angry at—it was the version of Him I'd been taught to believe in. The one shaped by culture, sermons, and upbringing. Growing up Nigerian, I was raised to think prayer was a transaction: if you are faithful, God will answer. If He doesn't, you must not have prayed hard enough. No one ever said that sometimes prayers go unanswered—and that this doesn't mean God has failed.

So when my mum died despite my pleading, it wasn't just grief that broke me—it was disillusionment. I had been taught to expect certainty when faith was always meant to hold mystery.

But in truth, faith—and life itself—*is* mystery. Sometimes prayers aren't answered, and we don't know why. Sometimes there's no explanation. Real faith lives with that uncertainty and still holds on.

Looking back now, I can see that my anger came from being misled by interpretation, not by divinity itself. Maybe God understands that too—that my frustration was never disbelief in Him, but heartbreak in the way I was taught to expect Him.

Some people find faith deepens after tragedy. They say suffering brings them closer to God. I understand that, but it isn't my story.

For me, losing my mum exposed a painful paradox: if God exists and has the power to intervene, He chose not to. If He doesn't have the power, what's the point of prayer? If He doesn't exist at all, then I'd been speaking to empty air for twenty-two years.

The loss of faith was a second death. Not only was my mum gone, but the framework I used to understand life and meaning collapsed too. I had to rebuild—not just my routines, but my worldview.

This is rarely spoken of, especially in Black and religious families where faith is seen as unquestionable. To lose belief after trauma feels like betrayal. But it isn't. It is a natural response to having your entire understanding of the world shattered.

Some people eventually return to faith, in a new form. Others, like me, build meaning elsewhere—in kindness, love, and human connection. *Both are valid paths back to light.*

What I Built in Place of God

When faith left, I didn't collapse into nihilism. I built something else.

I believe in the universe now—in karma, in luck, in the simple truth that treating people with kindness creates meaning all on its own. I don't need divine oversight to know what's right. I just try to be a good person, at all times. Try to stay positive. Try not to wish anyone harm, even when they've hurt me. That's how I live at peace.

My morals became my religion: treating people right, being kind, not misleading or betraying anyone, staying loyal. These aren't commandments from above; they're choices I make because they feel true.

Being an orphan gave me a strange kind of freedom. No parents to tell me I'm wrong for losing faith. My brothers don't care much. Timi and Tony talk about God sometimes, but they don't push. Strangers might say I shouldn't have lost my belief—but it is what it is.

I even had a friend's sister try to convince me to believe again after my mum died. She was insistent, almost desperate to save my faith. Then she lost her own mother. Now she doesn't believe in God either. She apologised, saying, *"I'm so sorry. I can relate to you now."*

Loss has a way of revealing what's real.

I don't go to church. I'm not against it. If a friend asked me to come for something important, I would go. But I don't seek it out. I no longer celebrate religious holidays the way I used to.

Here's what I can't fully shake: I was raised Christian, taught that God was real and that prayer worked. That conditioning doesn't disappear overnight. So yes, sometimes the word slips from my lips, or I think it in old habits—but that's all it is, a habit.

If there is something out there, it isn't the God I was promised. Not the one who answers prayers. Not the one I trusted that day in the bathroom. *That God died with my mum.* What remains is just the question mark—and I've learned to live with uncertainty instead of pretending I have answers I don't.

What I believe now is simpler: consequences exist. Science exists. If you walk into traffic, you'll get hit by a car—not because God wills it, but because physics exists. Kindness matters because we're all we have. Love matters because it's the only thing that lasts.

Losing faith doesn't mean losing meaning. I can live with compassion and purpose without believing in divine oversight. I can still marvel at beauty, still feel gratitude, still commit to love.

The God of my childhood left me on 7 July 2012. But I remain—still breathing, still capable of love, of hope, of joy.

And perhaps that's enough.

When God Felt Like a Stranger

Allowing myself to grieve the loss of belief alongside the loss of my mum felt necessary. Both absences deserved acknowledgement.

Pressuring myself to reclaim faith when it didn't feel real only deepened the wound. Meaning can exist without the divine.

Seeking community with others who understand the loneliness of losing faith after loss helped me feel less alone.

Building new frameworks for meaning—through love, kindness, and human connection—gave me ground to stand on.

Most importantly, this truth: questioning is not betrayal. My doubts are valid, even if my community doesn't understand.

For You, If You're Angry at God

How has loss affected your relationship with faith, spirituality, or belief in divine care?

What framework for meaning have you built to replace what no longer feels true?

Do you feel pressure from others to maintain faith despite your doubts?

What still feels sacred to you, even if traditional religious belief doesn't?

Perhaps faith was never meant to be certainty. Perhaps it was always this—choosing to love, even in the absence of answers.

Love Remains

"Faith may fail, but love remains. Even when the God I knew left me, life itself whispered: keep breathing, keep loving, keep going."

Chapter Eleven

Crossing Oceans to Outrun Memory

"Geography cannot heal what distance cannot touch."

I fled London because everywhere I looked, I saw her.

Standing at the window, waiting for that little yellow car to pull up. Watching her walk towards the house after parking. Our trips to the grocery shop, our drives to get our eyebrows, hair and nails done. The house itself carried her in every room, every corner soaked in her presence.

The UK had become a museum of memory, and I couldn't bear to live inside it.

Nigeria felt like escape. I convinced myself that living somewhere her shadow didn't follow would make grief manageable. In London, everything reminded me of my mum. In Lagos, I could walk down any street without triggering a flashback, sit in cafés that held no shared history, exist in spaces that were mine alone rather than ours.

The cultural shift felt like protection. In London, friendship required careful navigation: asking permission to visit, scheduling intimacy, maintaining polite distance. But in Nigeria, in Africa, friends are like family. You can show up unannounced. You can live with them for a while. You can seek comfort without formal invitations.

I thought that kind of warmth would heal me. I imagined myself surrounded by the easy affection of Nigerian friendship, cocooned in community, too busy laughing and living to dwell on loss. I thought geographical distance from her memory would translate into emotional distance from the pain.

I was wrong. Grief packed its bags and followed me across continents.

The panic attacks that had started in Soho continued in Lagos. The sleepless nights that plagued me in London became sleepless nights under Nigerian skies. The depression, the mood swings, the strange habit of disappearing from social situations, all of it travelled with me like faithful, unwanted companions.

But now I was dealing with it in isolation, far from the few people who knew what I was carrying. Only Deby and Joy really understood about the panic attacks before I left, and Joy knew the most. She had been my midnight refuge, the person I called when terror convinced me I was dying.

"eloho, are you sure you want to leave now, when you're still having panic attacks?" Joy kept asking. "Why not wait until you feel a bit better?"

But I was certain. "No, I'll be fine," I told her. "I think the panic attacks will stop once I get to Nigeria—there's too much life there, too much chaos, too much warmth. It'll distract me. I'll be surrounded by people. I won't have time to panic."

I believed that. I thought the noise and closeness would drown out the fear, that the thought the warmth of Nigeria would steady my heartbeat.

In Nigeria, none of my friends knew. They didn't know that when I went quiet during conversations, I was fighting to stay present. They didn't know that when I suddenly left parties or disappeared for days, it wasn't rudeness, it was survival.

I had expectations Nigeria couldn't meet. My friend Ese did live with me for a while, and I thought her presence would fill the void my mum had left. I imagined having her around would make the loneliness easier to bear—that somehow, together, we could soften the silence that had settled over my life.

But grief made me difficult to be around. I was sharp, withdrawn, unpredictable. Life had its own rhythm, and when she eventually left, it wasn't her fault; it just reopened the wound I'd been trying to heal. I told myself I understood, yet a part of me still felt that familiar ache. I felt the ache of loss all over again. The emptiness returned, familiar and sharp.

I felt abandoned all over again.

The Night I Couldn't Outrun Fear

The worst night came when all my coping strategies collapsed. I lived in a flat-style apartment and usually slept in my friend's room, sharing her bed for comfort. That evening—however—she decided to spend time with the man she was dating.

Normally, when panic struck, I would sit with the gate men—the security guards at the compound where I was staying. They thought I was just being friendly and social, unaware that I was clinging to their company to keep my terror at bay.

But this night was different. The panic was crushing. *Nothing could hold me together.*

I took an Uber, circling the island aimlessly. Esse was too far away, and the hour too late for safe travel across the city. The driver grew frustrated as I directed him in endless loops, desperate to escape the fear consuming me.

In the end, I called a man I had been on a date with earlier that evening. "*Can I come spend the night at yours?*" I asked, knowing how strange it sounded since I'd already declined his invitation hours before.

When I arrived, he offered me a separate room, but I couldn't bear the thought of being alone. "*Please, can I sleep in the same bed with you?*" I asked, my voice trembling, too panicked to care how it looked. He hesitated—a mixture of surprise and quiet apprehension crossing his face—but he nodded anyway.

I wasn't thinking of romance or intimacy. I was thinking about survival. I was convinced I was going to die that night, and I couldn't bear the thought of dying alone—with strangers who wouldn't know how to contact my family, who wouldn't understand what was happening, who couldn't provide the kind of care I thought I needed.

I wanted to die safe, if I had to die. I wanted to die beside someone educated enough, worldly enough, to handle the situation properly. To call the right people. To treat my death with dignity rather than confusion.

That was the night I realised fear could make you reach for anyone who made the world feel a little less unbearable.

What Geography Never Promised

That night crystallised a truth I had been avoiding: grief had followed me to Nigeria. The panic attacks, the depression, the overwhelming loneliness, none of it had been left behind in London. The only difference was that in Lagos, nothing reminded me of my mum directly. But the absence was just as loud. The ache was just as present.

I realised then that I hadn't been running towards healing, I had been running from memory. But you can't outrun what lives inside you. Grief isn't geographical. It's cellular, woven into your nervous system, embedded in your ways of moving through the world.

The streets of Lagos didn't trigger the memories the way London did, but they couldn't cure the underlying reality: my mum was gone, and no amount of distance could change that.

This recognition was both devastating and liberating. Devastating because it meant there was no escape, no place on earth where grief couldn't find me. Liberating because it meant I could stop running. I could start learning to live with what I carried.

Geography taught me this: healing doesn't happen through avoidance. You can't escape grief by changing your location any more than you can escape your shadow by walking in a different direction. The work of integration, learning to live with loss, has to happen wherever you are.

The irony is that Nigeria did teach me something valuable. Not about outrunning grief, but about the universality of human kindness. The gate men who welcomed my company, the friends who opened their homes, the stranger who let me sleep safely through a night of terror, all of them showed me that care exists everywhere. That even in the midst of profound loss, love still appears in unexpected forms.

But the deepest healing couldn't come from external sources. It had to come from within. From learning to be present with my own experience. From stopping the run, and listening to the grief that only existed because I had loved her so much.

Nigeria couldn't cure me. But it taught me that survival doesn't always look the way you expect. Sometimes it looks like gate men who don't know they're saving you. Sometimes it looks like a stranger offering you a safe place to sleep. And sometimes it looks like finally understanding that the only way through grief is to stop running from it.

In the end, I chose to leave Nigeria and return to London. I couldn't survive the distance from the life I knew; the echoes of grief were too heavy to bear alone. Coming home didn't mean I was constantly surrounded by friends or family, but knowing they were within reach—*just a cab, train, or short ride away*—felt like a small tether to safety, a quiet closeness I hadn't had across the ocean.

Now I live in London, still navigating grief, still building a sense of home from the pieces I can reach.

Why Distance Couldn't Save Me

Geographical change won't cure emotional pain. Healing happens from within, not from without.

Noticing what I was running towards versus what I was running from helped clarify my needs. Both motivations are valid, but they require different care.

Building support systems wherever I am became essential. I couldn't expect a new location to provide them automatically.

Letting disappointment guide me towards my real needs taught me something valuable. When escape doesn't work, you discover what actually might.

Most importantly, seeking comfort is not weakness. Sometimes survival takes you to unexpected places and people.

For You, If You're Running From Grief

What were you hoping distance would cure that it couldn't touch?

How did changing your environment teach you what grief really is?

What unexpected kindness appeared when you tried to escape?

What did you learn about yourself when running away stopped working?

Grief Travels Light

"You can cross oceans, change continents, start fresh in new cities, but grief travels light. It needs no passport, requires no visa. Healing happens not when you escape it, but when you stop running and learn to carry it with grace."

Chapter Twelve

Anticipatory Grief: Say It Now, Before It's Too Late

"Anticipatory grief is proof of love. It hurts because you care."

In Nigeria, I thought distance would heal me. It didn't. Running from memory only taught me this: grief follows you everywhere—but so does love. What helped, eventually, wasn't escape; it was learning to speak before silence became permanent. *Healing begins the moment we stop running from what hurts and start naming it.*

Fear of losing someone can sit heavy in the body. Restless nights, racing thoughts, a chest that feels too tight. This is anticipatory grief: mourning before the goodbye has even arrived. It is the heart's way of saying, I know what's coming, and I am terrified of the day I can't hear them, see them, or reach them anymore.

Sometimes this fear comes from watching someone age or fade from illness. Other times it arrives without warning—a sudden terror that anyone you love could be gone tomorrow. A partner in a car accident. A friend lost to suicide. A parent who seems perfectly healthy today. Death does not wait for old age or hospital beds. The fear is not always about gradual decline. Sometimes it is simply about the fragility of life itself.

It hurts because you love them. The ache before loss mirrors the bond you carry now. *Fear, in its own way, is love trying to protect what it cannot keep.* You cannot stop the future from arriving, but you can choose what to hold in the present: their laughter, their voice, their stories, the shape of their hand in yours.

The Grief Before the Goodbye

Most people don't have a name for what they're feeling when they lie awake at night: terrified of losing someone who's still alive. They think they're being dramatic, morbid, or pessimistic. They carry the fear in silence, convinced no one else understands.

But this fear has a name. It's called anticipatory grief. And it's as real as the grief that arrives after loss.

Anticipatory grief is the mourning that begins before death. It's the tears you cry whilst someone is still breathing. The panic that rises when you imagine a world without them. The questions you suddenly need answered. The stories you urgently want to record. The desperate need to memorise their face, their voice, their presence whilst you still can.

It's grief and love existing in the same breath. And it's exhausting because you're trying to live fully with someone whilst simultaneously preparing for a future without them.

If you're feeling this, you're not broken. You're not being morbid. You're simply awake to the reality that love and loss are inseparable. And that awareness, though painful, can also be a gift. It reminds you that time is not guaranteed. That today matters. That the people you love deserve to be told, shown, and celebrated now, not later.

What I Lost

When my mum died, I realised how much I hadn't captured. I lost the curve of her handwriting. I lost her recipes, especially the famous beans only she made the way it should be made, her quiet family speciality.

I wished I had asked more about the stories she carried, the details of her childhood, even the medical history I assumed I would learn one day. I wished I had learned the secret of her beans, the recipe never written down because she believed we had years to cook it side by side. I wished I had told her more often how much I loved her and taken every chance to gather her wisdom whilst she was still here to share it.

I miss the small, intimate moments too. I miss plucking the hair from her face whilst she begged, *"eloho, please, can you come and pluck my hair from my face? They're growing out."* I always took my time, teasing like a child, pretending to delay it, but of course, I did it. I miss the rhythm of her calls and the way she insisted I do it properly, the gentle persistence that was both loving and exasperating. I miss watching her sit in the living room, reading her Bible—the quiet focus of her devotion.

I miss us watching television together, how she screamed and yelled at every twist and turn, and how I'd tell her off, laughing, "*Mum, shush, calm down*! *Shush, calm down*!" even though I secretly loved every moment of it. Especially when she was watching football—shouting passionately at the screen, sometimes yelling "*ṣí gba*! *ṣí gba*!" in Yoruba. I didn't even know what it meant back then; but now, reflecting and writing, I've had to ask my friends, who explained that she was probably shouting at the opposing team to "*play rubbish*" or "*mis-kick.*" It makes me smile now—the thought of her yelling in pure passion, lost in the game, her voice echoing through the room like music I can never forget.

Every unshared recipe, every forgotten story, every little moment now gone feels like a small fracture in the life we had together.

I lost the exact sound of her laugh, the way her voice softened when she said my name.

I had a handful of photographs and no videos. Those small details seemed ordinary whilst she was here. When she was gone, they became treasures I would have traded anything to recover.

At twenty-two, I was certain I had decades left to gather what mattered. I pictured long afternoons with questions and tea, me taking notes whilst she cooked. I did not imagine a clock running out. My mum died suddenly. Healthy one day, gone the next. I thought she had years ahead of her. Death did not wait for old age. It did not give warnings. It simply arrived.

Back then, social media held fewer memories. Instagram was new. Facebook was for updates, not archives. No one I knew was sending or saving voice notes, or filming ordinary moments. That absence still aches. I wish I had filmed her cooking, captured her just being herself in everyday moments, recorded her voice saying my name the way only she could.

I cannot go back for those things. That is why I refuse to dismiss the ache that arrives before goodbye. *Anticipatory grief is not wasted pain. It is an invitation.* What if you spoke the words you keep postponing? What if you gathered what might matter later? What if you loved them loudly now, so your future grief has something soft to lean on?

What I Wish I Had Saved

Video and audio recordings of her laugh, the way she said my name, her voice when she spoke softly.

Even one short video of her cooking those beans, the way she stirred, tasted, and adjusted seasoning without ever measuring, would have meant everything.

Just one page in her handwriting, hidden in a book somewhere—a fragment of her I could still touch and remember, as if touching her.

Ordinary videos that weren't staged—her telling a story, humming in the kitchen, laughing at something on TV, trying to wake me up in the morning and telling me not to be lazy.

Family stories recorded in her own voice. Who came before her, what they lived through, what she wanted me to remember.

I wish I had filmed us together—me telling her how much I appreciated everything she did; how she fought for me and my brothers, raised us alone, guiding us from the streets of Nigeria to new beginnings in London—fighting every obstacle to keep us close, and carrying all the struggles of our lives. I wish I had told her how much I admired her strength, how deeply I looked up to her, and how much I cherished her for never giving up on us.

The Fear of Loving What You'll Lose

When the fear and ache rose in my chest, I learned to slow my breath and focus on the memories I could hold onto.

I close my eyes and remember the laughter we shared, watching TV together, the little jokes, the ordinary moments full of love. I reflect on her voice, the way she called me "sweetheart," "my love," "honey," and how her words shaped me into who I am today.

I look at the few photos I have of her on my phone, one by one, letting them remind me of her presence. I listen to the voice notes my brother sent me, the small "hello" messages, just to hear her voice again. I think about the calls she used to make, the way she checked on me, the tiny gestures full of care.

Focusing on these memories (her laugh, her words, her love) helps me carry the ache. It doesn't take it away, but it softens it.

SayItKit

In the years after she died, I kept meeting people who carried the same regret: I wish I had said more, saved more, asked more.

Slowly, I began to build a gentle way to make it easier. A simple set of prompts and letters I call the SayItKit. It isn't a programme or a performance; it's a bridge between I wish I had and I'm saying it now.

It holds space for the everyday love we forget to record whilst we still can.

What follows is not instruction. It's a record of what I wish I had done, and what I now try to do whilst the people I love are still here.

For You, If You're Already Afraid

Ask yourself: What do you want to tell them that you've been holding back?

Which ordinary moments should you film and record whilst you still can?

What questions do you wish you could ask about their childhood, their health, their hopes, their regrets?

Which keepsake would have meant the most to you: video of their voice and movements, audio of their laugh, their handwriting, their recipes, their stories?

What about you? If you're reading this whilst the people you love are still here (your parent, your partner, your sibling, your friend), what do you want to make sure you don't lose?

Say It Now

The fear you feel before goodbye is not weakness. It is love bracing itself. Let it guide you towards presence rather than paralysis.

They are here now. Their voice is within reach. Their hand is still warm. Their laughter still lives in the next room.

If you can, say it now. Film them now. Record them now. Ask the question. Write the note. Make the soup together, take the trip you keep postponing, and film the way they season by instinct. Do what you can whilst you still can.

When the day comes, your grief will sit beside the treasures you chose to gather whilst you still could.

The Gift of Now

"What if you said it now, before it's too late? What if you filmed them today, recorded their voice, asked the question you've been holding back? They are here now, and that is a gift you can still choose to honour, if you can, when you're ready."

If you are reading this book before loss has arrived, and you want to understand more deeply what it means to carry this fear and how to prepare your heart, turn to the closing section **"For Those Who Fear Loss"** at the end of this book. It was written specifically for you.

Chapter Thirteen

The Envy of the Living

"Jealousy in grief is not hate or cruelty. It is the ache of love that cannot return."

No one warns you how jealousy weaves itself into grief like a thread you can't untangle. For me, it wasn't the random posts from strangers on social media, or glossy family portraits I could scroll past without blinking. It was the moments closer to home: the graduations, the weddings, the family gatherings, where absence shouted loudest because I knew what it should have looked like if my mum were still here.

At my own graduation, I broke. My brother, Timi, had convinced me to go, and he came with me. The drive there was the worst, my mind spinning with everything I knew I would face. I didn't want to go, but he insisted. I already knew what to expect, rows of students, some with families, some without, and I needed my mum. My mum had promised me my first car when I graduated. She was everything: my world, my anchor. The thought of her absence was unbearable.

Sitting there, watching rows of students with their mothers, mums fixing gowns, taking photos, beaming with pride, it was unbearable. I cried through what should have been a milestone. My brother didn't ask questions; he just sat beside me, offering quiet comfort. He could feel my pain without words, and he kept saying softly, "It's okay, don't worry, I'm here." I couldn't bring myself to take a professional photo. I had to leave.

The drive back home was even worse. Every tear, every thought of all the mothers and children laughing and celebrating reminded me of what I had lost. A day that should have been triumphant felt hollow, like joy with its heart ripped out.

Family gatherings were no easier. My mum's sisters looked so much like her that being around them was like pressing on a bruise. At barbecues or birthdays, their presence reminded me of what I no longer had. For years, I avoided them as much as I could, because every hug felt like reopening the wound.

But grief has a way of surprising you. Earlier this year, at my cousin Alika's wedding party, I saw my aunt—Aunty Mary, my mum's sister—and something shifted. Hugging her that day felt different: less like pain, more like healing. For the first time, it felt like I was holding my mum again.

Later that evening, I posted a photo of us together on my story on Instagram and captioned it:

"Sometimes being around family, especially the ones who look like her, makes the absence louder. But seeing my auntie felt like looking into my mother's eyes again, and for a moment, I didn't feel the ache, just the warmth."

That moment didn't erase the years of avoidance, but it reminded me that even in absence, presence can return in unexpected forms.

Social media, oddly enough, hasn't cut me as sharply as real life. A stranger posting their mother doesn't shake me. Every now and then, when someone I know posts about their mum, it still stirs something in me. But even then, social media has become a quiet outlet for me—a space to express love when words need somewhere to go.

I don't rant or pour bitterness into captions. Instead, I sometimes write about my mum on her birthdays and anniversaries. It's where I sometimes take to honouring her, releasing what sits heavy in my chest—where I let love spill out in words to the world. Sometimes posting is how I remind myself that she lived, that she mattered, that she still shapes me.

Envy in grief isn't about cruelty. It's longing in disguise. At first, it made me resentful: seeing intact families, watching friends laugh with their mothers, knowing I would never have that again. Over time, I learned to let those pangs guide me. Envy meant I still wanted her. It meant love was still alive.

When Grief Distorts Empathy

Another shadow of comparison is how grief can temporarily distort your empathy. Not in a cruel way, but in a survival way. When your own world feels unbearably heavy, it can shrink your ability to hold space for someone else's pain.

I caught myself thinking: *but your loss isn't as deep as mine* when people grieved breakups or job losses. It wasn't hatred. It was my own grief narrowing my capacity to see beyond my pain.

I remember when Esse mentioned she had lost a friend recently. Each time she cried, I looked at her quietly and said, "*It's okay, you'll cry forever. It's all right.*" But deep down, I found myself thinking, at least she still has her mum and dad. In my mind, her loss felt smaller—as if she hadn't yet touched the kind of pain that hollowed me out.

In time, I learned to meet people where their pain lives. Every grief feels total to the one carrying it. For some, it's a breakup or a friendship lost; for me, it is my mum.

And not everyone's grief looks like death. Some people grieve homes lost to fire. Some grieve the version of themselves they used to be, or the life they thought they'd have. Others grieve safety, love, health, or time itself. Grief wears many faces, and every one of them is valid.

Grief isn't a competition. There's no scoreboard, no hierarchy of pain that makes one person's suffering more valid than another's. Remembering this softened the edges of comparison and helped me return to compassion—both for others and for myself.

The Phone Call That Never Comes

My mum used to call me so often it *felt like twenty times a day*

Not because there was an emergency. Not because something urgent had happened. Just because she wanted to hear my voice. To check in. To make sure I was okay. To tell me she loved me. *Again.*

If I ignored her call back in Nigeria, she'd call my friends to find me. When I moved to London and I was at work, she'd call my workplace if I didn't pick up. She was overly caring, overly affectionate, impossibly present. And sometimes, honestly, it annoyed me.

I'd answer the phone with irritation in my voice. *"Mum, what? We literally just spoke."* And she'd respond in that sweet, gentle voice of hers: *"eloho, my love, I'm just checking in on you. Just making sure you're okay."*

I never had the chance to call her. She never gave me the opportunity. She was always the one reaching out, always the one initiating, always the one making sure I felt loved and seen. My phone rang constantly—morning, afternoon, evening—multiple times, every single day.

I didn't realise how much I needed that until it stopped.

The Silence

Now, my phone doesn't ring.

Thirteen years later, the silence is deafening. No one calls to check if I'm okay. No one texts just to say they're thinking of me. No one reaches out twenty times a day to make sure I'm still breathing, still standing, still here.

And every single day, that absence reminds me she's gone.

It's not just about missing her. It's about missing the feeling of being checked on. Of being someone's priority. Of knowing that somewhere in the world, someone is thinking about you constantly, worrying about you, making sure you're not alone.

My mum was a caller, not a texter. She wasn't a tech person. She didn't send messages or emojis or voice notes. She picked up the phone and dialled. And now I don't even have old text messages to read back. I don't have a record of her love in writing. I only have the memory of her voice, and even that is starting to fade.

When I reach for my phone now, it's not to call her. I know I can't. It's just the reflex of looking at it and thinking: no one's going to ring. No one's going to check in. The person who used to call me constantly is gone, and no one else has filled that space.

Because no one else can.

The Love That Can't Be Replaced

I've said this before, and I'll say it again: no one loves you the way your mother does.

Friends and family check in occasionally, text on birthdays. But no one calls me several times a day just to check in. And if you're grieving your mother, you probably know this feeling too. No one loves you the way a mother does. No one worries about you the way she did. No one makes you the centre of their world the way a mother does.

Since my mum died, I've been reminded of that every single day. Not in grand, dramatic ways. In small, ordinary moments. In the silence of my phone. In the absence of someone asking, "*Are you okay? Have you eaten? Did you sleep well?*"

Every day, I'm reminded that no one loves me like that anymore. And it's not anyone's fault. It's just the reality of loss. Some loves are irreplaceable—and a mother's love is one of them.

What I Wish I Could Ask Her

If I could call her now, what would I say?

Everything. Anything. All the small, insignificant things that don't feel small when you have no one to share them with.

Life decisions. *Should I do this? Should I have done that? Mum, I'm sick—what should I do? What would you do?*

My mum had answers to everything. Not because she was all-knowing, but because she knew me. She understood me in a way no one else ever has.

I wish I could go on holiday with her. Create memories. *Be girls together.* Talk about men, about dating, about life. I wish I could call her when I'm upset, or when something exciting happens, or when I just need to hear her voice telling me it's going to be okay.

Every basic, simple question. Every piece of advice. Every ordinary conversation. *I miss all of it.*

People ask, "*What do you miss most?*" And the answer is: *everything.*
I miss *everything.*

The Places That Hold Her

Her physical absence is everywhere, but some places hold it more than others.

When driving past Pimlico, Vauxhall, Victoria—the areas where we used to live—I feel it. I point it out to my brother: "*This always reminds me of Mum.*"

But honestly? *Everything* reminds me of her. There's no *small* thing that triggers the memory. It's not just certain places, or certain dates, or certain moments. It's every day. *Every single day,* something reminds me she's not here.

A conversation I wish I could have. A decision I wish I could ask her about. A moment I wish I could share. The absence isn't occasional—it's constant.

And I don't think that will ever change.

Living with the Silence

Thirteen years later, I still miss her calls. I still wish my phone would ring and it would be her, checking in, making sure I'm okay, telling me she loves me for the twentieth time that day.

But it won't. It never will. And I've had to learn to live with that silence.

If you're grieving someone who used to check on you constantly, someone whose love felt suffocating in the best way, know this: the silence is one of the hardest parts. It's not dramatic. It's not a single moment of collapse. It's just the daily, quiet ache of knowing no one will ever love you that way again.

And it's okay to miss that. It's okay to feel the absence every single day. It's okay to wish your phone would ring.

Because some loves are so big, so overwhelming, so impossibly present, that their absence is felt in everything.

And that's not weakness. That's just proof of how deeply you were loved.

When Everyone Else Had What I Lost

Envy in grief isn't pettiness. It's not bitterness or ingratitude. It's the raw, unbearable ache of watching others hold what you'd give anything—everything—to have back, even for five minutes.

In the early years, right after she died, I turned away from Mother's Day posts and muted the noise of other people's celebrations. I couldn't bear the reminders.

Before she died, I'd always connected easily with my friends' mums—I'm family-oriented by nature, and I liked knowing their families, their warmth, their stories. But after she was gone, that stopped completely. I couldn't bring myself to say hello anymore or build those connections again. I didn't want to hear the sound of another mother's voice or feel the warmth I'd lost. It wasn't anger—it was ache, and maybe protection too. If I got close, it would only remind me of what I no longer had.

I still avoid gatherings where daughters sit beside their mums like it's the most ordinary thing in the world.

That ordinariness—that ease—still feels like a knife.

But envy taught me something I didn't expect: it showed me the shape of what I lost. The intensity of my jealousy revealed the depth of my love. I wasn't envious of strangers with mothers I'd never met. I was grieving the irreplaceable presence of mine.

Some loves cannot be substituted. No amount of friendship, therapy, or time will fill the space a mother leaves. And pretending otherwise—telling yourself to *"move on"* or *"find closure"*—only dishonours what was real.

The silence my phone holds now is permanent. No one will ever reach for me with that relentless, suffocating, beautiful constancy. And I've had to stop apologising for missing what can never be replaced.

Envy isn't the enemy. It's love turned inside out, searching desperately for the person it belongs to. And when you can't find them, you see their absence reflected in everyone who still has what you don't.

That jealousy?

It's just the measure of what mattered.

For You, If Everyone Else's Normal Hurts

Have you ever felt envy in grief, longing for what others still have? How did it manifest for you?

Are there moments or events—birthdays, graduations, weddings—where absence hits hardest? How do you navigate those feelings?

How has grief affected your ability to empathise with others' struggles, even temporarily?

What rituals, memories, or acts help you honour the person you lost and transform envy into love or remembrance?

How do you balance feeling your own grief while witnessing joy or celebrations in others' lives?

When you see someone with their mother, what does your envy tell you about the love you carry—and the space it still holds in your heart?

The Wisdom in Envy

"Jealousy in grief isn't cruelty—it's love with nowhere to land. With time, you learn not to measure your ache against anyone else's. Your grief is already enough, your love already complete."

Chapter Fourteen

The Regret That Teaches

"Regret is love in disguise. We only regret because we cared."

If you are reading this before loss has arrived, let these regrets guide you. You still have time to ask the questions, record the voices, and say the words. Do not wait.

The regret from that morning haunts me still.

My mum often asked me to do the simplest things with her: dinner together, shopping side by side, even getting our hair done at the same salon. I usually said no, too caught up in my twenty-two-year-old life to understand that these invitations were gifts I was casually throwing away.

I thought I had time. I thought she would always be there, patient and available whenever I finally decided to show up properly. Instead, I chose my friends almost every time. She would tease me gently, "You carry your friends on your head like Òsùká."

Òsùká: a Yoruba word for the folded cloth women place on their heads to carry heavy loads. She meant it as gentle teasing: you prioritise your friends like a weight you balance above everything else, including your own family. She was right, and now that truth sits in my chest like a stone I can't dislodge.

I regret the things I didn't ask, the stories I never heard, the quiet lessons I didn't notice. I regret not learning the secret of her beans—her best dish, the family speciality she never wrote down because she trusted time would stretch ahead for us. I regret not telling her often enough how much I loved her, and not gathering her wisdom while she was still here to share it.

I regret not telling her how much I appreciated her sacrifices—how much I admired the way she fought for me and my brothers, how she always put us first. I regret not expressing gratitude for the countless ways she gave, protected, and shaped our lives.

I regret the small moments I took for granted: the way she laughed at nothing, the rhythm of her morning routine, the stories she told me without realising they were lessons. I regret the afternoons I didn't linger just to watch her move through her day, the conversations I let slip away thinking there would always be tomorrow.

Every unasked question, every untold story, every quiet gesture I failed to notice now weighs heavily, a reminder that time is finite, and some things, once lost, can never be retrieved.

The Anger I Couldn't Name

"When love had nowhere to go, it burned"

For a long time, I couldn't admit this: I was furious at my mum.

Not at God. Not at the world. At *her*. For leaving me. For dying too soon. For breaking her promise about buying me my first car. For not holding on long enough to see me grow older, steadier, stronger.

In the beginning stages, the anger was white-hot. I didn't understand. She just left me. No goodbye. No warning. No preparation. Nothing.

She died of a sudden aneurysm. One moment she was here, teasing me through my bedroom door at 3 AM. The next, she was on the bathroom floor, and then she was gone. No sign. No chance to brace myself. No time to say the things that needed saying.

I was so angry. So confused. *Why would you let yourself die? Why didn't you fight harder? How could you just leave me like this?*

I resented her. I thought: *So you just decided to die and leave me? Wow. That's crazy.*

The anger leaked out everywhere else. I was cold. I was cruel. I snapped at people who didn't deserve it. I walked away from conversations mid-sentence. I lived in a fog of rage I couldn't name because admitting I was angry at my dead mother felt like the ultimate betrayal.

Now, thirteen years later, there's still anger. But it's not as deep. It's softened into something closer to sadness, to acceptance, to the recognition that she didn't choose to leave. Death chose for her.

But in those early years? I was livid. And I had nowhere to put it.

When I Needed My Mum Most

"Lockdown turned absence into emergency"

In 2020, I made a decision that felt like progress: I moved out of my brother Timi's house and into my own place. For the first time in my life, I would live alone. It felt like a milestone, like I was finally adulting properly, standing on my own two feet.

Then the pandemic hit.

And suddenly, living alone wasn't freedom. It was isolation. The world locked down, and I was trapped inside four walls with nothing but my grief and my thoughts for company.

That's when the uncontrollable tears started.

Not the dramatic, sobbing kind. Not the kind where you wail and scream and collapse. These were different. They were silent, relentless, unstoppable—tears that ran down my face for weeks, for months, without pause. I would wake up crying. I would eat crying. I would sit on the sofa staring at nothing, and the tears would just keep coming.

My friends would call me or see me with tears streaming down my face.

"eloho, what's wrong? Why are you crying? Did something happen?"

And I'd say the same thing every time: *"I'm just missing my mum, wishing she was here. My mum is not here. That's the issue. Why is she not here?"*

Because that was the truth. There was no dramatic incident, no specific trigger, no new trauma. It was just the crushing, suffocating weight of her absence pressing down on me whilst the entire world was also falling apart and I had no one to turn to.

Years after the pandemic, while we were talking about everything I'd gone through back then, my friend Esse reflected on what I'd been like. She said: *"You kept saying the clouds are dark, everywhere is dark and gloomy. I kept telling you to turn on the light, but then I realised you weren't talking about your house. You were talking about what was happening inside your head."*

I don't even remember saying those things. My mind was so consumed by darkness that I was vocalising my internal chaos without realising it. The walls felt like they were closing in. The world outside my window looked grey and oppressive. But it wasn't the weather or the lighting. It was grief, manifesting as a physical weight pressing down on everything I saw.

This was different from the grief I'd carried since 2012. I'd always needed my mum. Every single day since she died, I'd wished she were here. But the pandemic was the first time I really, really needed her. Not in the abstract, existential way. In the urgent, desperate, "I need you NOW" way.

If she had been alive, I would have been with her. I wouldn't have been alone in that flat, crying into the silence, terrified to fall asleep because sleep meant I might not wake up. I would have been safe with her, the way I'd always been safe with her.

But she wasn't here. And I couldn't go to my brothers because I was angry at them for reasons I can't even fully remember now. The anger was so intense that even when I was drowning in panic, even when I called the ambulance on myself three times because I was convinced I was dying, I still couldn't bring myself to ask them for help.

The panic attacks during the pandemic were the worst I'd ever experienced. My chest would lock up. My heart would race so violently I could hear it in my ears. I was certain, every single time, that this was it. That I was going to die alone in that flat, and no one would find me for days.

I called the ambulance three times. Three separate occasions where I was so convinced death was coming that I dialled 999, shaking and breathless, begging them to save me. One time, I was convinced I was having a stroke. The paranoia was so intense that every physical sensation felt like proof of impending death.

Each time, they told me the same thing: panic attack. Not a heart attack. Not a stroke. Not dying. Just panic.

But knowing didn't make it stop. The fear was absolute. The loneliness was unbearable. And my mum's absence, which I'd been living with for eight years by then, suddenly felt fresh and raw all over again.

The sirens outside didn't help. Every time an ambulance or police car passed by, the sound would trigger another wave of panic. My body would tense, my chest would tighten, and I'd be right back in that spiralling terror, convinced I was next.

I started eating compulsively. Not because I was hungry, but because eating was something to do, something to focus on besides the fear. I would finish an entire pack of Fruit & Fibre in one sitting—what should've lasted days, gone in minutes, just trying to fill the emptiness inside me with something, anything.

I gained weight. My body changed. But more than that, my mind was unravelling.

Eventually, I couldn't take it anymore. When restrictions eased slightly and we were allowed to stay with one person outside our household, I packed my things and went to stay with my cousin Tare for two months. I needed to not be alone. I needed another human presence in the house, even if they couldn't fix what was broken inside me.

Most days at Tare's, I cried. He would look at me, concerned, confused, probably exhausted by my constant tears.

"*Why are you crying?*" he'd ask gently.

"*I don't know,*" I'd say. *But I did know. I was crying because if my mum were alive, I wouldn't need to be here. I would be with her. I would be safe.*

After a couple of months, I knew I couldn't live alone again. Not like that. Not in that isolated, terrifying way. So when I moved out of Tare's house, I found flatmates. That's when I started living with flatmates, a decision that would become essential to my survival.

I didn't need them to talk to me or hang out with me. I wasn't capable of socialising or engaging in conversation. I just needed to know someone was there. Someone in the next room. Someone whose presence I could sense through the walls, whose footsteps I could hear, whose existence meant I wasn't completely alone.

Having flatmates gave me a safety net I desperately needed. I would stay in my own space, in my own room, but knowing there was someone next door made me feel safe. *It was a small kind of peace, but peace nonetheless.*

From my window at the back of the house, I could see our cosy garden—a small patch of green that felt like its own little world.

In the middle stood a tall, beautiful palm tree, rare for London, its leaves swaying softly in the wind. There was something about it that calmed me. The stillness, the movement, the way it caught the light. Every time I looked out, I felt a kind of serenity I hadn't known in months. That palm tree became my quiet therapy—a reminder that even in unfamiliar soil, something could still grow tall and steady.

Sometimes, I'd hear my flatmates sitting outside, smoking and talking late into the night, their laughter drifting up through my window. It reminded me that life was still happening, even in the quiet.

Next door, our neighbours would often sit out in their garden too—the fence between us low enough that our conversations carried easily from one side to the other. One of them played the guitar sometimes, the sound floating softly through the evening air. I'd watch from my window, listening, feeling a strange peace settle over me.

It was such a contrast to the months I'd spent alone, staring out at empty streets and silence that felt endless. Now, when I looked out the window, I saw life again, and it felt like company.

Even with those moments of calm, the fear still lingered beneath the surface. If my flatmates were going to be out for the night, I would have to leave too. I'd go stay with someone else, anyone else, just to avoid being alone in that flat. The thought of spending a night by myself was unbearable.

The pandemic taught me something brutal: grief doesn't fade with time in the way people think it does. Eight years after losing her, I was still capable of being completely undone by her absence. The loneliness, the fear, the desperate ache for her presence, it could all come roaring back as if no time had passed at all.

And in that isolation, with the world shut down and everyone trapped in their own terror, I learned that some griefs are simply unbearable without the person you lost. You can survive them. You can get through them. But you cannot make them lighter. You can only endure.

That was the pandemic for me. Not just a global crisis. A personal reckoning with how much I still needed my mum, and how unbearable it was that she would never, ever be here again.

The Regret That Stayed

"Some stones the heart never puts down"

Most of all, I regret not going back into that bathroom to hold her hand.

She was lying on those cold tiles, breathing hard, and I ran to call for help—which was right—but I didn't return to reassure her that she wasn't alone in her terror. That moment haunts me more than any other.

Years later, my brother's question still echoes: *"eloho, why didn't you just pick her up and drive her to the hospital yourself? You can drive. Why did you wait for the ambulance?"*

At the time, I didn't know how to answer him. I was petrified. I knew what I was seeing was bad—really bad. My body froze. Fear rooted me to the spot, and all I could do was call for help and then stand in the hallway, praying to a God I would soon stop believing in.

I know now that I was twenty-two, terrified, and doing the best I could in an impossible situation. But regret doesn't care about logic; it only knows what it wishes had happened.

Even if I had done everything perfectly, even if I'd carried her myself to the hospital, she might still have died. The doctors, the ambulance, the hospital—they couldn't save her either. My regret wants to believe I had power I didn't actually have. It wants to believe her death could have been prevented if only I had been enough. But some things are beyond our control, no matter how much we love.

The Moment I Stayed

"This time, I didn't run. I stayed. I held her hand"

Years later, one of my friends attempted suicide.

I got the call and rushed to the hospital. When I arrived, she was on the bed, breathing heavily, her body convulsing from the cleaning products she'd ingested. The doctor immediately told me to leave the room.

I refused.
"I'm not going anywhere," I said.
"You need to leave now. This is not appropriate for visitors."
"I'm not leaving."

The doctor insisted. I started crying. Then I started screaming.

"My mum died the same way! I ran away from her! I left her alone! I'm not doing that again! I'm staying!"

I was hysterical, but I didn't care. I held my ground. The flashbacks were overwhelming—my mum on the bathroom floor, me in the hallway, too scared to go back to her.

"I wish I had held my mum's hand! I wish I had told her I was here and loved her! But I ran away and left her alone! I'm not doing that again! I'm staying!"

Eventually, the doctor relented. They let me stay. I held my friend's hand. I whispered to her that she wasn't alone. I refused to leave her side until she was stable.

Although we are no longer in each other's lives, I was there for her that day. I fought for her. I did for her what I couldn't do for my mum.

That moment didn't erase my regret, but it taught me something: I will never run away again. If someone I love is in crisis, I will be there. I will hold their hand. I will tell them they're not alone.

My mum's death taught me that lesson in the hardest way possible.

But at least it taught me.

What Has Softened, What Hasn't

"Time is sandpaper, not a solvent"

Thirteen years later, some regrets have softened. I'm no longer as hard on myself. I understand now that I was young, inexperienced, unprepared for trauma of that magnitude.

I can say *my mum passed away* now without feeling like it's an insult to her memory. For years, even acknowledging her death felt like betrayal.

I allow myself to be happy now. In the beginning, happiness felt like disloyalty, like moving on meant forgetting her. I've learned that joy and grief can coexist. That loving my life doesn't mean I loved her any less.

But the regret about not holding her hand? That one hasn't softened. Talking about it now, even after all these years, makes me feel the weight of it fresh and raw.

I don't think that regret will ever fully leave. It's woven too deeply into the fabric of that day, into the image of her on those cold tiles, into the knowledge that I could have been braver.

The only thing that eases the pain is this: I was young. I didn't have experience with trauma. My body went into freeze mode, and I did the best I could with the tools I had.

That doesn't make it okay. But it makes it human.

What Regret Taught Me

"Regret is love's way of reminding you what matters most"

Regret taught me that love and loss are inseparable. I regret so deeply because I loved so completely. The two are bound together, and one cannot exist without the other.

It taught me that I needed to speak the words I was holding whilst people were still here to hear them. That's why I created the SayItKit: so others might avoid carrying the weight of unsaid things the way I do.

It taught me that some regrets will never fully heal. They become part of you, shaping how you love, how you show up, how you hold the people who remain.

Most importantly, it taught me this: you can carry regret and still move forward. The weight doesn't have to crush you. It can become the soil where new purpose grows.

The Words I Never Said

"Let hindsight become instruction, not punishment"

Reframing regret as evidence of love helped. When I catch myself spiralling into "I should have," I try to shift to "I loved in the ways I knew how then." Hindsight is clarity I didn't have at the time.

Regret can guide present choices. When I catch myself holding back love, I remember this feeling and choose differently.

Writing down my regrets instead of letting them consume me made them manageable. On paper, they're quieter, less powerful, easier to hold.

Using regret as a teacher rather than a tormentor changed everything. It showed me what mattered. It showed me how to love better. It showed me that time is not guaranteed.

And this truth: even when regret whispers that I failed, love whispers back that I tried. And trying, even imperfectly, is its own kind of love.

For You, If Regret Won't Let Go

What is one regret that still echoes for you, and how could you reframe it as proof of love rather than proof of failure?

How has regret shaped the way you love the people who are still here?

If you could go back, what would you say or do differently? And what does that tell you about what you need to say or do now?

Presence Over Perfection

"Regret taught me that love doesn't need perfection to be real. It just needs presence. And even when I couldn't be present in that bathroom, my love was still there. It always was. Regret cannot erase that truth, no matter how loudly it tries."

Chapter Fifteen

Rituals That Anchor

"Rituals are what we build when natural order collapses"

At first, grief felt like a gaping absence screaming from every corner of my life. I hid photos, silenced memories, stayed away from traditions that felt too heavy to bear. I thought avoiding reminders would protect me.

But avoidance wasn't protection. It was just another way of drowning.

When my mum died, the world became formless. Panic attacks, sleepless nights, the collapse of my faith left me craving structure. I needed something tangible, predictable, safe. I needed ritual.

Rituals are the anchors we build when the natural order of life is destroyed. They are not about magical thinking or forgetting. They are deliberate acts of honouring love when nothing else makes sense.

My Rituals Are Not What You'd Expect

I don't cook her favourite meals. That feels performative, not true to who I am or how I grieve.

I don't visit her grave. I tried twice, maybe three times. The last time triggered panic attacks that lingered for years and still visit sometimes. The cemetery became a place my body refused to return to, and I stopped forcing it.

I don't write her letters. That's not my language.

My rituals are quieter, rawer, more unconventional. They live in my solitude.

The Ritual of Quiet Moments

"Stillness became the language she could still hear me in"

About a year ago, maybe late 2023, I started noticing something. When I retreated into my quiet indoor moments—what I used to call my "depressed episodes" but now recognise as something else entirely—I wasn't just isolating. I was connecting with my mum.

For thirteen years, I distracted myself. Gym, travel, friends, socialising, networking. Always moving, always busy, never still. I thought that's what survival looked like: constant motion to outrun the grief.

But a year ago, I discovered something revolutionary: *stillness is also a ritual.*

When I choose to be alone, when I say no to plans and stay in my quiet space, I'm actually spending time with her. My mum knows I'm not just out there living life and forgetting her. She knows I'm thinking of her. Feeling her absence. Honouring the weight of what I lost.

That's my biggest ritual—the quiet indoor moments. The solitude I once feared and now crave. It's how I stay connected to her when the world feels too loud and her absence feels unbearable.

The Ritual of Vocalisation

"Speaking her name aloud reminds the silence it's not in charge"

Sometimes, when I'm alone, I speak to her out loud.

"I miss you, Mum."

"Why did you have to leave me?"

"Life sucks without you."

These are my rituals. They're not polite conversations with the universe. They're raw, unfiltered, grief-soaked declarations thrown into the silence of my room—into the space where her voice should still exist.

Sometimes I cry when I say them. Sometimes I scream them. Sometimes I whisper them so softly the air barely carries the sound.

But speaking them out loud makes her feel less gone. It turns absence into presence, if only for a moment. It gives my grief a voice instead of letting it rot quietly inside me, unsaid.

The Ritual of Heavy Crying

"Some releases arrive only through tears"

Once or twice a year, the heavy cry comes—the kind that shakes your whole body, the kind that leaves you breathless and spent.

I used to fight it. Now I welcome it.

My birthday last year was intentional solitude. I chose to be alone, unaware that the heavy cry would come. And when it did, it felt like release—like my body finally exhaling grief it had been holding for months.

Allowing myself to feel, fully and without distraction, is a ritual. It's my way of saying: this pain is real, this loss matters, and I will not pretend otherwise.

The Ritual of Music

"Every song is a bridge to the place where love still lives"

Music became another way to stay connected to her.

I listen to Nightbirde's *"It's Okay"* when I need permission to fall apart—when I need to remind myself that it's okay not to be okay right now, when grief feels like it's sitting heavy in my chest and my body needs to breathe it out.

Dean Lewis's *"Memories"* and *"How Do I Say Goodbye"* when missing her feels unbearable, when the ache of her absence presses so hard I can barely remember my own breath. The songs let me grieve out loud, even as I clutch the hope that somewhere, she's listening.

Ed Sheeran's *"Visiting Hours"* when I wish I could visit my mum one more time—to tell her everything I never said, to sit beside her and let her hand hold mine, to feel the warmth of her presence for just a moment longer.

Celine Dion's *"Goodbye's (The Saddest Word)"* when the finality of her passing feels impossible—when I need the music to remind me that love doesn't vanish with a farewell, that even in silence, it continues to move through me.

There are many other songs I turn to, but these are some of the ones that let me feel her absence without being consumed by it. Music gives my grief a language when words fail. It carries the pain I cannot speak aloud.

Sometimes I play these songs and cry. Sometimes I simply listen and remember. Sometimes I scream them out loud—in pain, in agony, and sometimes with tenderness. These are my rituals. They keep her close.

The Ritual of Writing

"Writing turned grief from wound into witness"

I started journalling on 30 November 2024, my birthday. It was the first time I allowed myself to write about grief fully, without holding back or censoring what I felt. I'd often typed fragments of thoughts into my iPhone notes before, but that day was different—it was the first time I sat down to truly journal, to pour everything out intentionally.

Since then, I've poured months of energy into words—this book, my thoughts, my pain, my survival. Writing has become how I keep her memory alive, not through polished tributes or Instagram captions, but through honest, messy, unfiltered truth about what it is to live without her.

I have used the SayItKit as part of this process, letting prompts and exercises guide me and uncover feelings I did not realise I was holding. This book itself is part of that ritual: a space to honour her, to bear witness to my grief, and to turn absence into something tangible, something that survives even when she cannot.

Since that first page, writing has become a lifeline. Each word, each sentence, each unfinished paragraph is a conversation with her, a way to carry her presence forward in the world, and a reminder that even in loss, love can still speak.

The Rituals I Don't Have

"Absence can be a ritual too"

I don't always post about her on social media. Sometimes I do. Sometimes I don't. I acknowledge her birthday, her death anniversary, but not always publicly.

Lately, I've been enjoying being more private. The world doesn't need to know what I'm doing or how I'm grieving. That privacy is its own kind of ritual—protecting my grief from performance, from expectation, from anyone's judgement but my own. I'm not saying I'll never post again—I just follow how I feel. And lately, I haven't felt the need to share.

I don't do grand gestures either. No long epistles that live on my feed. No yearly tributes written for applause. When I share, it's usually a quiet story that disappears in twenty-four hours—fleeting, like memory itself. Some families host annual memorials or gather at graves, others design headstones and hold services each year. There's nothing wrong with that. My grief just doesn't need ceremony to be sincere.

We haven't even placed her headstone yet—not out of neglect, but because we're still finding the strength to face it. For some, ritual is structure; for us, tenderness arrives in its own time. We remember her in other ways—in laughter, in stories, in silence.

I don't follow traditional expectations of mourning. I don't set annual traditions or fixed commemorations to prove I remember. Some years I speak. Some years I stay silent. The love is constant either way.

I also haven't turned my home into a shrine. No altar of photographs. No framed portraits on the wall. I can't even put my mum's photo up yet. I keep her pictures on my phone—and when I need to, I look at them. But having her face on my wall still feels too heavy, too raw.

A few years after she passed, when I stayed at my brother Tony's house, I remember he had her photo by his bedside. I couldn't bear it. I turned it face-down and asked him how he managed to sleep beside it every night. Even now, thirteen years later, I still can't.

Recently, during a conversation about my mum, my auntie Mary asked, *"Why wouldn't you have your mother's photo up on your wall or on your table? Why wouldn't you want to look at the woman who sacrificed everything for you?"*

I told her it's not about avoidance or lack of gratitude. It's about readiness. Having her face on my wall feels like reopening a wound that hasn't healed. Maybe one day I'll be able to. But right now, I can't.

I'm not saying I'll never have her headstone made or visit her gravesite. I'm not even saying I'll never frame her photo and place it by my bedside. I'm just following how I feel—moment by moment, year by year.

Because grief doesn't obey calendars or customs. It only asks for truth.

The truest rituals are often invisible.
The rituals I don't have are still rituals.
Unseen, unspoken, but deeply alive.

Rituals Don't Need to Be Grand

"The smallest acts often carry the greatest love"

For years, I thought rituals had to look a certain way—candles lit beside framed photos, fresh flowers laid at gravesides, anniversaries marked with family gatherings or long, emotional posts online. I thought honouring someone meant doing something visible, something everyone could recognise as love.

But my rituals are private. Unconventional. Sometimes they may seem like depression to outsiders, but to me, they are connection.

Quiet moments alone. Speaking her name into the silence. Heavy cries that leave me lighter. Writing to make sense of what I feel. Choosing solitude over socialising, because solitude is where I meet her.

These aren't the rituals grief books tell you to create. But they're mine. They work. They hold me. They carry me. They keep her close.

What Rituals Have Taught Me

"Rituals don't end the ache. They give it rhythm"

Rituals should serve you, not obligation. If lighting a candle comforts you, light it. If it deepens your ache, don't. The ritual only matters if it is true to your grief.

Some rituals keep memory alive. Others help you move forward while still carrying them. Both are valid. Both are necessary. Both can coexist.

Rituals don't keep grief alive—grief is already alive, stitched into your being. What rituals do is keep love visible. They give shape to what cannot be spoken, a language for what still lives inside you.

In the beginning, I wanted grand cures—something dramatic enough to match the size of my loss. But it was the smallest rituals that saved me: sitting in silence, playing one song until my heartbeat slowed.

Grief didn't ask for miracles; it asked for presence.

Each act, repeated quietly, became a way of telling myself I was still here, still trying. Over time, I realised healing wasn't a single revelation, but the gentle return to tiny mercies—done again and again until they felt like home.

Surviving the Calendar

"The calendar remembers even when you try to forget"

The calendar doesn't forget, even when you wish it would.

Mother's Day. Her birthday. Christmas. 7 July. My own birthday. These dates circle back every year, relentless and unavoidable, each one carrying the weight of her absence.

I used to sometimes spend those days with my cousins—gathered together, surrounded by family, trying to fill the space she left.

It helped, for a while. Being around people made the day feel less empty, less impossible to survive. But over time, something shifted.

I realised that being around other mothers on Mother's Day, or celebrating Christmas in houses full of laughter and maternal warmth, wasn't comforting anymore. It was painful. It reminded me of exactly what I was missing. The absence became louder, not quieter.

So I changed my rhythm. For the past few years, I've spent Christmas with my brothers and my nieces—knowing we're all in the same boat—or sometimes I spend it alone, curled up in bed catching up on a series. It's not about isolation; it's about surviving the day with as little pain as possible. It isn't sad. It's actually warm when we're together, and quiet when I'm not. We don't always acknowledge her on Christmas Day. Maybe this year we will. Maybe we won't. I honestly don't know.

Mother's Day and her birthday (10 April) come with their own weight. Some years I post about her on social media. Some years I don't. Sometimes I just speak out loud: *"I miss you. Happy birthday, Mum."* Sometimes I say nothing at all. Before I launched my podcast, I released a Mother's Day video encouraging people to text their mothers, take them out, appreciate them whilst they're still here. Because life really is too short. But acknowledging the day for myself changes year to year.

I don't visit her grave anymore. The last time I went, it triggered panic attacks so severe that I couldn't breathe. That day broke something in me, and I decided I wouldn't go back. My grief doesn't live at a gravestone. It lives everywhere—in me, in my memories, in the moments I wish I could call her and can't.

But the hardest days? My birthday and 7 July.

7 July is the anniversary of her death, and it ruins me every

single year. Even before July arrives, I can feel the heaviness creeping in. The sadness doesn't announce itself. It just settles over me like a cloud, and suddenly I'm grieving her all over again as if no time has passed at all.

July is always hard—her death month. My energy dips, my mood sinks, and I dread the approach of the 7th. I have no ritual for July except survival. *Every day, every hour, every breath becomes the work of enduring.* Still, I'm trying to find a way to face it differently—to create something small, something honest, that honours her without reopening every wound. Maybe one day, that too will become a ritual.

In the early years, I distracted myself. I made plans. I surrounded myself with friends. I drank a little. I refused to sit still long enough to feel the weight of that day. I couldn't bear to be alone with my grief, so I ran from it.

But over the past few years, I've done the opposite. I stay by myself on 7 July now. Sometimes my friends text me. I usually ignore them. Not because I don't appreciate the gesture, but because I don't want people acknowledging the day. It feels awkward. We already know what it is. There's no need to say it out loud.

I don't have set rituals for these dates. I don't light candles or visit places we used to go. Sometimes I pretend it's just another day. Sometimes I don't. Mostly, I'm just sad. I cry. I miss her. And I let myself feel it without trying to fix it or escape it.

My own birthday is somehow worse.

It's a trigger I didn't expect. My birthday reminds me that I'm getting older and she's not here to see it—that I'm living years she'll never witness. Every milestone, every achievement, every version of myself she'll never meet.

For years, I distracted myself on my birthdays too. I travelled. I celebrated with my cousins. They would host me, gather around me, make me feel loved and held. And it worked. It kept me from sitting in the sadness.

But last year, for the first time, I spent my birthday alone in Nigeria. I didn't plan anything. I didn't distract myself. I just sat with the grief. And I cried like I had just lost her—deep, ugly sobs that made me wonder if I'd make myself sick. The first time I allowed myself to really feel the weight of her absence on that day instead of running from it.

This year, I'm doing something different. I'm going on my first solo trip to Madeira, Portugal, for my birthday. Not to escape the grief, but to sit with it somewhere beautiful. To honour the fact that I'm still here, still living, even though she's not.

Christmas, as I said, has become easier. Being with my brothers and my nieces makes it feel warm instead of hollow. But Mother's Day, her birthday, 7 July, and my own birthday? Those still hurt. They probably always will.

What I've learned is that there's no right way to survive these days. Some years you post about them. Some years you stay silent. Some years you surround yourself with people. Some years you need to be alone. Some years you acknowledge the grief. Some years you pretend it's not there.

The calendar will always bring these days back. But how you meet them can change. And that's okay.

If you're dreading a date that's coming, know this: however you choose to survive it is valid. Whether you distract yourself or sit in the sadness, whether you talk about it or stay silent, whether you're with people or alone, you're doing it right.

Because surviving is enough. *And some days, it's everything.*

For You, If You're Searching for What Helps

"There is no wrong ritual. Only what keeps you here"

What ritual, however small or unconventional, connects you most strongly to the person you lost?

Do you feel pressure to grieve in ways that don't feel true to you? What would it look like to honour them in your own language instead?

Which traditions or days feel unbearable, and how might you protect yourself without guilt?

Quiet Acts

"My rituals are not grand gestures. They are quiet acts of defiance against a world that expects me to move on. They are proof that love does not need presence to remain visible. It only needs me, still here, still speaking her name into the silence."

Chapter Sixteen

When Purpose Returns

"The weight you carry can crush you, but it can also become the soil where new purpose grows."

In the beginning, grief felt like a stone on my chest: too heavy to move, too suffocating to survive. People told me, "One day you'll find purpose in this pain." Instead of comfort, those words felt like pressure. Purpose sounded like a test I was failing. I wasn't building anything. I was barely breathing.

In those years, I resisted the whole idea. I didn't want her death to become a project or a mission. I didn't want to make it worth something. I wanted her.

But slowly, without planning, small cracks appeared. The first time I spoke her name without breaking. The first time I wrote one sentence in her voice. The first time I shared a sliver of my grief with someone instead of hiding it like shame.

These weren't grand gestures. They were survival. But survival carried her forward, and that was its own kind of purpose.

The Fire That Went Out

Before she died, I had fire. I wanted to act, to present, to be seen, to succeed. I was ambitious, driven, hungry for a future shaped by external validation. Fame. Recognition. Wealth. Proving I'd made it.

When she was gone, that fire went out. Ambition felt pointless. Why dream if life could end so suddenly? Why chase success when the one person who believed in me most wouldn't be there to see it?

For years, the only thing I was consistent in was grief. I moved through days like a ghost, present but not alive, breathing but not living. Purpose felt like a luxury I couldn't afford when survival was taking everything I had.

When Purpose Changed Shape

"Purpose no longer shouted. It whispered: live gently"

Thirteen years later, something stirred. But it wasn't the old fire returning. It was something quieter, deeper, more honest.

Purpose stopped being about what I could achieve and became about how I wanted to live.

It became about human connection. Not networking or performance, but genuine, messy, imperfect relating. Showing up for people who showed up for me. Letting go of relationships that required me to shrink or perform.

And here's what surprised me: it also became about not chasing connection. Not forcing friendships. Not fussing over family relationships that drain me. I used to believe that love meant constant effort, constant reaching, constant maintenance. Now I know that real connection doesn't require force. It flows naturally, or it doesn't flow at all.

It became about kindness. Not the polite, people-pleasing kind that drains you. The kind that includes kindness to myself. The kind that says: I matter too.

It became about authenticity. Saying yes when I mean yes. Saying no when I mean no. Not going above and beyond for people who wouldn't walk halfway for me. Not burning myself out to prove my worth.

It became about boundaries. Protecting my energy. Choosing where to spend my limited capacity. Understanding that "*no*" is a complete sentence, and guilt is optional.

It became about health. Not the gym obsession that kept me running from grief, but actual wellness. Rest. Sleep. Saying no to stress. Recognising that life is too short to sacrifice peace for productivity.

It became about positivity. Not toxic optimism that pretends pain doesn't exist, but choosing to focus on what I can control. Surrounding myself with good energy. Cutting out negativity that doesn't serve me.

It became about selfishness. The healthy kind. The kind that says: my needs matter. My time matters. My mental health matters. Choosing myself isn't betrayal. It's survival.

It became about feeling. Allowing emotions to move through me without judgement. Crying when I need to cry. Resting when I need to rest. Not apologising for being human.

But most importantly, it became about loving myself. Truly loving myself.

For years, I said the words. "I love myself. I love myself." I'd look in the mirror and tell myself I was beautiful, hot, worthy. I meant it too. I genuinely believed I loved myself. I knew my worth.

But those were outward declarations. Surface-level affirmations. Words I could perform.

I was loving myself externally, performing self-love, but not truly internalising it. I wasn't living it in the quiet moments when no one was watching. I wasn't treating myself with the tenderness I desperately needed. I wasn't doing it intentionally.

Now I'm discovering what it means to love myself inwardly. Deeply. In the marrow of my bones. In the choices I make when no one's looking. In the grace I give myself when I'm struggling. In the rest I allow myself without guilt.

This is the self-love that actually matters. Not the Instagram caption kind. The unglamorous, unsexy, deeply necessary kind that chooses you even when choosing you feels uncomfortable.

The Paradox That Saved Me

"Losing everything made me see what was already mine"

Here's what I didn't expect: losing my mum killed my ambition but gave me clarity.

The old me wanted success to prove something. To matter. To be seen.

The new me knows I already matter. Not because of what I achieve, but because I'm still here. Because I survived. Because I chose to keep living even when living felt impossible.

That's purpose—not the shiny, Instagram-worthy kind, but the quiet, unglamorous kind that whispers: *you are enough, exactly as you are, even on the days you achieve nothing at all.*

Some days my purpose is creating. Other days my purpose is resting. Both are valid. Both hold value.

If You Feel Purposeless

If you feel passionless, confused, or empty, it isn't because you are broken. Sometimes it's grief. Sometimes it's life—the weight of routine, disappointment, transition, or unmet expectations. Both can dim your fire for a while.

Grief steals ambition, clarity, energy, time. But so can burnout, heartbreak, or simply existing in a world that keeps demanding more. It can blur years into survival mode.

You are not failing. You are living through something that would stop anyone.

Connection helps. Sometimes it's peers who understand. Sometimes it's professionals who can untangle the knots. Reaching for help isn't weakness. It's a sign you are still searching. And searching is courage.

Purpose doesn't announce itself with fanfare. It whispers—through survival, through the choice to keep loving, keep living, keep carrying forward what matters most.

Some days, surviving itself is purpose. Every day you wake up and live again, you carry love forward. That's the victory.

What I Built From the Ruins

"Purpose arrived when I stopped searching for it"

Not rushing helped. Purpose emerged naturally when I stopped demanding it.

Noticing what broke through numbness gave me clues: a song, a sentence, a small moment of connection. Those pointed towards what mattered.

Seeking professional support when the weight felt unbearable wasn't weakness. It was me choosing to keep going.

This reminder helped: survival is enough. Some days, that alone is my purpose.

Most importantly, releasing the pressure to "make something" of my grief freed me. My mum's death doesn't need to produce anything. It already produced the most important thing: it taught me how to live.

For You, If You're Searching for Meaning

What did purpose mean to you before loss? And what does it mean now?

Have your values shifted from external achievement to internal peace, or is your journey different?

What would it look like to stop forcing purpose and let it emerge naturally?

The Quiet Revolution

"Peace became the prize I never thought to chase"

Purpose didn't return the way it left. The old ambition died with my mum. What grew in its place was quieter but stronger.

I don't chase fame anymore. I chase peace.

I don't work hard anymore. I work intentionally.

I don't prove my worth anymore. I protect it.

That shift, from external validation to internal peace, is the purpose grief gave me.

From Doing to Being

"I used to measure purpose by what I built. Now I measure it by how I feel when I wake up. Do I dread the day or do I breathe easier knowing I'm living in alignment with what actually matters? That shift—from achieving to being—is the quiet revolution grief gave me."

Chapter Seventeen

The Second Season

"Survival was the first decade. The second is learning how to live. They are not the same task, and that is why you feel lost again."

The New Classroom

No one told me grief comes in seasons.

This second season has surprised me in ways I never imagined. For the first time in my life, I went four days without showering. Even when my mum first died, I never experienced that. I always told myself I could never let things go that far, but here I was. I still cleaned myself, but the act of standing under water felt impossible. It wasn't neglect—it was grief pressing down until even the smallest routines became mountains.

I used to see images and videos online of people speaking about this—homes untidy, days without bathing—and I thought, that could never be me. But grief has a way of humbling us. It shows how even the simplest acts of care can crumble when the weight is too much. It isn't filth. It isn't laziness. It's another language grief speaks through the body.

The first season was chaos: panic, hallucinations, sleepless nights. I survived that storm. But graduation does not mean freedom. It only means a new class begins.

The second season is quieter, but it cuts just as deep. It is not about her death anymore. It is about what has died in me. Confidence. Drive. The untouchable girl who once believed nothing could stop her.

I am not drowning anymore, but I am drifting. I am not always sleepless, but mornings ache with questions. I am not hallucinating, but I am paralysed by purpose.

If the first decade was survival, this one is reconstruction. And reconstruction is a brutal teacher.

Somehow I Blinked and I'm 35

"Grief has no calendar—but one day you wake up, and a decade is gone."

I spent more than ten years conquering sorrow: the decade of panic attacks, hallucinations, sleepless nights, unstoppable tears, depression, and the constant fear that I was losing my mind. That was phase one of grief, and it nearly destroyed me.

But I fought. I survived.

And yet, somehow I blinked—and I'm 35. Thirteen years later, I am still lost, not in the chaos anymore, but in the aftershocks. Not drowning, but drifting. Not screaming, but paralysed by silence.

Smiling With Cracks

Outwardly, I look like I'm thriving. I manage projects. I speak about ambition. I move through the world with a straight back and a steady tone. People see competence.

Inside, I'm still 22. The year she died.

My ambition froze with her. She was the grit in my blood—the woman who worked endlessly, raised children without a man, and never gave up. She was the whisper that told me, you can do this. When she died, that whisper died too. In its place grew a void.

If she had stayed just a little longer—until I was 25 or 26—I might have planted my feet before the earthquake came. Instead, she left me half-formed, still light, still careless. And now, at 35, I sometimes feel like a child pretending in an adult body, trying to catch up to a life that should have been mine.

The Aftershock at 35

"The shaking stops eventually—but nothing ever looks the same again."

I watch my friends thrive in ways I haven't managed to yet.

They're getting married, having babies, buying homes, climbing career ladders with steady focus. We talk about our lives openly, not in a bragging way, just sharing passions and goals the way close friends do. They're private people, so none of this plays out on social media. It's real conversation, intimate sharing.

And I'm genuinely happy for them. They're building the lives they want.

But it holds up a mirror. It shows me the version of myself I might have been if 7 July, 2012 had been an ordinary Saturday. The version who kept that fire burning instead of watching it get buried under thirteen years of just trying to survive.

My friends know I'm different. I chose freedom over stability. I'd rather earn less money and have the ability to travel, to up and go tomorrow if I wanted. They earn more but have responsibilities: babies, mortgages, commitments that require planning. Neither path is better. We just made different choices shaped by different losses.

When my mum was alive, I felt unstoppable. Like I could conquer anything, achieve everything, because she was my God, my protector, the voice that said you can do this before I even knew I needed to hear it.

Now I'm cautious. Because if anything happens, there's no one I can really call. No one can be there for you like a mother. That safety net is gone, and I move through the world knowing I'm working without one.

So watching my friends thrive doesn't make me jealous of their babies, homes, or careers. It just reminds me of how much time I lost to survival, and leaves me with a quiet hope that maybe it's not too late to start really living.

Here's the truth—I probably would have wanted those same things if my mum hadn't died. I would have followed the same rhythm of life we're taught to desire—working, saving, building a home, ticking the usual boxes. But grief changed my compass.

Losing my mum shifted something fundamental. I'm not craving babies or marriage or the traditional path. Those aren't on my list of goals unless love finds me in a way that feels undeniable, and even then, I'm not sure. My dreams look different now: freedom, creating, writing, building something that matters, living in ways that feel true rather than expected.

Watching them thrive doesn't hurt; it only reminds me how long I've been paused while life moved forward.

The ache that runs deeper is simpler.

It comes when I'm sitting at dinner with friends and someone casually mentions their mum. A phone call they had. Advice they received. A visit they're planning. The conversation continues around me, but I'm not fully there anymore. I'm sitting with the ache of what I don't have.

Or sometimes when I'm with my aunties, my mum's sisters who look so much like her, and their presence reminds me so sharply of her absence that I've avoided them for years. Only recently, I am open to spending time with them again, to hug them and feel like I'm holding my mum once more, even if just for a moment.

That's the ache that never quiets.

Not my friends' milestones or their successes.
Not the glossy social media versions of other people's lives.

Just the intimate, unavoidable moments when someone mentions their living mother and I'm reminded: mine is gone, and no matter what I build or achieve or become, I will always be doing it without the person who was supposed to see it.

No one can be there for you like a mother. And that is the ache that sits with me every single day.

When the Mirror Stopped Reflecting

For thirteen years, I had a formula that kept me functional.

The gym. Travel. Socialising with friends. Nice restaurants. Burlesque shows. Live music. Rooftop bars. These were my sources of happiness, my self-care, my proof that I was still alive and thriving despite the loss.

Especially the gym. For thirteen years it was my anchor. I lived there five, six times a week. It gave me clarity. It steadied my mind. When panic threatened to consume me, I could burn it off with weights and treadmills. When sadness felt unbearable, I could sweat it out. The gym wasn't just exercise—it was my therapy, my ritual, my daily reminder that said: *You are still here. You are still strong.*

I thought these things would sustain me forever. I thought I'd found the magic combination that would carry me through the rest of my life.

Then, about three months ago, everything shifted.
The gym no longer felt like home. I struggled to go three times a week. Some weeks, not at all. The restaurants felt empty. Travel still excited me, but it no longer felt like an escape—it felt familiar, predictable, like another version of the same view. Even my friends—the people I never said no to, the ones I'd drop everything for—suddenly felt like too much.

I started saying no. For the first time in my adult life, I declined invitations without guilt eating me alive. I stopped checking in on people the way I always had. Not because I stopped caring, but because I was empty. The love tank that had fuelled all those years of showing up for everyone else was finally, completely drained.

At first, I felt guilty. *What's wrong with me? Why don't I want to go to the gym anymore? Why does the thought of socialising make me want to hide?*

Then I realised: nothing is wrong with me. Something is changing in me.

The Art of Slowing Down

"Rest is not retreat. It's remembering you are human."

For two months, I've been spending time with myself indoors. Just... being.

No agenda. No productivity. No performance. Just me, my bed, my series, my writing.

And here's the strangest part: it fulfils me. It actually makes me happy in a way the gym and the travel and the socialising used to, but don't anymore.

I'm discovering that all those things I thought were self-care were actually *external* self-care. They were activities, distractions, things I did to feel better. And they worked for thirteen years. They saved my life when I needed saving.

But what I need now is different. I need *internal* self-care. The kind that doesn't require movement or money or other people. The kind that's just... rest. Presence. Permission to exist without producing.

I'm learning to listen inward. To notice what I'm actually feeling instead of immediately trying to fix it or outrun it. To ask myself: *What do I need today? instead of What should I be doing today?*

Some days the answer is: absolutely nothing. And that's okay.

When Rest Felt Like Rebellion

"The body remembers what the mind tries to forget."

I haven't been to the gym in almost three weeks as I write this. It's not because I've been travelling, or sick. I've just... stopped. For no real reason other than not feeling called to go. Three weeks might not sound like much, but for someone who's been there religiously for thirteen years, it feels seismic.

The guilt tried to eat me alive. *Oh my god, I need to go. I need to go. The gym saved my life. How can I just stop?*

But then I caught myself. The gym did save my life, when I needed saving. When I was drowning in panic and needed somewhere to channel the terror coursing through my body. When grief was so loud I needed to exhaust myself into silence.

But I don't need saving anymore. I'm not drowning. I'm not using the gym as an escape. I'm just... not being called there right now.

And that's allowed. The gym will still be there when I want to return. But right now, what my body needs is rest, not exertion. What my mind needs is quiet, not the pounding music and adrenaline.

I'm learning that self-compassion means letting go of old rituals when they stop serving me, even if they once saved me.

My First Solo Trip—2025

In November, I'm going on my first solo trip. Ever.
For thirteen years, I told myself I could never travel alone. I needed friends. I needed company. I needed other people to make the experience worth it.

But spending these two months with myself has taught me something deeper. I've always enjoyed my own company, but this time it was different. I didn't want to engage with anyone or fill the silence with conversation. I wanted to sit with myself—fully, honestly—and *feel*. To finally give myself permission to *feel*, instead of constantly distracting myself.

So I booked the trip. Solo. Just me.

Last year's birthday taught me how healing solitude can be—how being alone doesn't have to mean being lonely. It showed me the quiet power of my own presence, the kind of peace that arrives when you stop running from yourself. Now I'm taking that same lesson into a new country: a whole week of just me, myself, and whatever grief or joy or peace decides to show up.

When Money Competed with Passion

I met Colette first.

She is one of those women who radiates order and ambition. She plans her life the way I make art: with precision and intention. She is grounded, structured, disciplined, and intentional. I have always admired that about her.

I am more of a live-in-the-moment, life-is-too-short kind of girl. She is the planner. I am the free spirit.

One evening, Colette invited me to dinner with her friends.

"Meet Barbs," she said. "She has been through loss too."

I thought the connection would be grief. But life had other plans.

At the table, Colette introduced me to Barbs.

"Barbs," she said, "you two should talk. I think you will get along. She lost her mum and she is launching a podcast on grief."

Barbs had lost her dad.

Before the grief conversation could even begin, Colette turned to another friend, linking them through work.

Barbs is a data scientist. She runs her own company. She is smart, sharp, full of energy. As the conversation flowed, Colette mentioned that Barbs also runs *Table4Thirteen,* a private members' social club for founders, entrepreneurs, and professionals. She hosts these incredible events, Colette said, laughing about how much Barbs invests in creating the perfect experience: sophisticated dinners, beautiful gifts, exceptional food. The kind of gatherings where connections are made over exquisite meals and genuine conversation.

The conversation around that table opened something in me. Hearing them talk so fluently about the business world—the strategies, the opportunities, the language I'd never mastered—felt like finally finding the door I'd been searching for. *It sounded like a language I used to speak and had forgotten.*

For some time, I had been brainstorming ideas with friends about how to make more money. Perhaps take a new course, learn a new skill. I had mentioned project management more than once, but deep down, I did not know where to begin. As a creative, I understood production, storytelling, building worlds, but when it came to the corporate world, I was lost.

That night felt like destiny. For months I had been asking the wrong people the wrong questions. And suddenly, here were two women who not only had the answers but were willing to share them freely.

When I mentioned my idea, Colette and Barbs almost said it together.

"No, not project management."

"Business analysis suits you more," Barbs said, breaking it down as if she were teaching a class. She talked about systems, communication, problem-solving, the art of interpreting data. Colette joined in too, using all the business terms I had never heard before, talking about the software, the pay, the kinds of companies that would hire me once I had finished the foundation course.

Between them, they had the insight, the connections, and the confidence I had been craving. *I could feel an old engine turning over inside me, reluctant but alive.*

"This is you," Barbs said with certainty.

Colette smiled and nodded. "Exactly. You would be brilliant at it."

For the first time, I felt seen in a new way. Not just as a creative, but as someone who could actually do this, if I wanted to.

Barbs, though a new friend, was incredibly open. She said, *"Text me any time. Ask questions. You can always come to my house. I'll show you how I work, help you prepare for interviews. I'm always happy to help."*

Colette encouraged it too. *"Make sure you call her. She's brilliant. She'll give you a hand."*

Their encouragement felt rare—*women confident enough in themselves to lift another woman up.*

A few weeks later, I decided to pursue it. But since I was already doing something I wasn't truly passionate about, I thought I might as well challenge myself in another way too.

I could have paid for a structured course with classroom training. That's how I learn best. That's where I thrive. But I chose to self-study instead. I was already trying something completely new—business analysis, a world I'd never imagined myself in—so I thought, *why not study in a new way too?* Push past my comfort zone and see if I could learn differently.

A challenge on top of a challenge.

Honestly, I had no real passion for it at first. What did I know about business? Almost nothing. But as I learned, I realised the process mirrored what I already did in TV production: research and planning like pre-production, gathering and interpreting data like production, and presenting insights like post-production. Suddenly, the course made sense, and I saw how my skills in storytelling, organisation, and connecting pieces could translate perfectly.

I thought, *maybe I can do this after all. But belief without desire is a quiet kind of friction.*

Deep down, it was not my passion. The only passion driving me was wanting more money.

I struggled. I am better at learning in a classroom, thriving on structure and accountability. But here I was, having to self-motivate without lectures, without deadlines, without anyone pushing me forward.

It did not work. I kept thinking, *I would rather be watching my series than studying this.* I could not even give up my series addiction for this course.

I tried. I kept trying. But it was not working.

Then something shifted.

I had filmed my podcast months earlier and left it sitting there, unfinished. But suddenly, working on that felt urgent. Real. *Mine.* I decided to channel all that energy into my podcast launch instead.

And here is what shocked me. My series were not a competition any more. Whilst I was preparing the podcast, working on the *SayItKit,* writing this book, I was not even thinking about series. They just stopped mattering. *Work that is mine calls softly,* and I go.

That was when I realised I needed to do what comes naturally to me. Something I am genuinely passionate about, not just a job that gets me money. My passion, with time, will bring me money.

Eventually, I told Barbs I wanted to focus fully on my creative work instead: the podcast, the *SayItKit,* this book.

She smiled and said, "*That is where your energy is. There is nothing better than doing something you love, something you are passionate about, and making money from it.*"

She was right.

A few weeks later, at one of Barbs' *Table4Thirteen* events, I told Colette that I still felt like I could be doing more. That maybe I had made a mistake stepping away from the course.

Colette just smiled and said, "*eloho, you have always known who you are. You love your work. You are not struggling. You can travel when you want, create what you want, and still live freely. Do not let the pressure of money take that away. You are not driven by it, and that is your strength. Keep following your passion.*"

Her words stayed with me. Because they were true.

I realised I was not unmotivated. I was just done forcing myself into shapes that did not fit me.

Colette reminded me to trust my rhythm. Barbs reminded me to build from what I love.

Money had tried to compete with passion. Passion won. Not because it is easier, but because it is honest. *Money is a metric. Meaning is a compass.*

Sometimes the right women do not just inspire you—they realign you with yourself.

Maybe the fire never died. Maybe it just changed form.

The Battle Between Who I Was and Who I'm Becoming

"Old fire, new peace—both live here now."

Here's where it gets complicated.

The old me, the go-getter who wanted to be famous, on TV, rich, successful—that version died with my mum. When she died, my values completely changed. I stopped caring about houses and cars and first-class flights. I started caring about health, presence, kindness, and the kind of rest my mum unknowingly sacrificed while she was busy holding us all together.

I developed a fear of working hard. My mum poured everything into us, and aneurysm took her without warning. She loved us with her whole being—so completely that she never saved enough of herself for herself.

So I learned to love differently. I learned to live differently. I stopped chasing, stopped running, stopped letting the world convince me that constant motion meant success. I started choosing ease over hustle, peace over pressure, stillness over noise.

But now, thirteen years later, something is stirring. The go-getter is trying to resurface.

I launched a podcast. I'm writing this book. I'm building the *SayItKit.* They are quiet acts of courage—proof that I'm beginning to want again; small signs that hope is stretching its limbs after a long sleep.

They come from someone who wants her work to be seen, felt, and to matter—but they also awaken the part of me that still flinches at the thought of overworking, of pushing too far, of repeating history.

Because in my body, drive and loss are intertwined. I watched my mum carry too much for too long, pouring herself into me and my brothers until there was nothing left for her. So even now, when I feel that same fire returning, it scares me.

I'm terrified. Because that hunger to do, to build, to achieve—it feels dangerous. It feels like the thing that took her away. It feels like loving too hard, giving too much, pouring until there's nothing left.

So I'm caught. I want to make more money. I want to build things that matter. But I don't want to lose myself trying to earn what I already have within me. I don't want to work myself into the ground. I don't want to mistake exhaustion for achievement.

How do you stay ambitious without breaking your own heart?

For a while, I didn't have an answer—just a feeling that something had to change. I didn't know it yet, but the healing had already begun. That question lingered in me for months, quietly rearranging everything I believed about ambition and peace.

The Quieter Kind of Lost

"Sometimes progress looks like stillness."

I've started to untangle this slowly—not through force, but through curiosity. By listening to what my body remembers, what my mind resists, what my heart still fears. Therapy will help me go even deeper, piece by piece, but even before that, I began learning how to sit with what hurts instead of running from it.

Then one night at 1 AM, unable to sleep and scrolling Instagram, I stumbled upon a clip from Dr. Sara Madani (from Dubai Bling). Her words stopped me cold:

'If you ask my friends, they'll tell you I'm the sweetest, the kindest. I'm always there for everybody, but I was not there for me. How does that make sense? I'm a hypocrite. How am I there for everybody but not for myself? How am I loving everybody but not loving myself? I thought loving myself was going to the gym, travelling, going to places. That's not self-love. That's taking care of the physical experience of life. When I come back from that destination, I'm sitting with my traumas again. Buying things is great, but when I'm bored of them, I'm still that broken person. Healing means I love myself enough to close a chapter and start a new one.'

I became elated. She'd cracked the code. I finally had an answer to what was wrong with me. It felt like she was speaking directly to the part of me that still carries my mum's exhaustion—the version of me that mistakes movement for meaning and calm for complacency.

Here's what I'm starting to understand: my mum died of an aneurysm. But the constant stress, the worry that consumed her, the burnout from never resting—her body carried more than anyone should have to bear. She was a worrier. She worked endlessly without breaks. She poured herself out for everyone else, especially me and my brothers, and never refilled her own cup. She didn't know how to rest, how to say no to us, how to protect her energy.

But I'm not her. I know what rest is now. I know what matters. I know that saying no to things that drain me isn't selfish. It's survival. My mum's strength built me. But my peace will sustain me.

So maybe the new version of success looks different. Maybe I can be ambitious and rest. Maybe I can want more money and not sacrifice my peace. Maybe I can hustle smart, not hard.

I don't have to work hard. But I can work intentionally.

That's the lesson of this second season. The first decade was about surviving the chaos. This decade is about learning how to live—how to build a life that honours both the drive I once had and the rest I now need.

The Go-Getter Is Not My Enemy

For years, I thought the ambitious version of me was dead and needed to stay that way. I thought wanting success made me dangerous—as if the same fire that drove my mum could one day consume me too.

But she's not my enemy. She's just scared. *Scared that loving her work too deeply will cost her everything again. Scared that rest means weakness, and drive means danger.*

The truth is, I can want success. I can build things. I can chase dreams. *Maybe healing isn't choosing one over the other. Maybe it's remembering that I can hold both—drive and rest, hunger and peace—without losing myself.*

As long as I do it my way. As long as I protect my rest. As long as I remember that my worth isn't measured by productivity.

The old me wanted to be rich and famous to prove something. The new me wants to create because it brings me alive. That's the difference.

What Steadies Me Now

"Joy looks different now—smaller, quieter, but still alive."

If someone asked me a year ago what made me happy, I would have said: the gym, travelling, socialising, burlesque shows, *dinners in candlelit restaurants and spontaneous nights out that felt endless,* savouring good food and better company, live music, rooftop bars, socialising with friends, trying new things.

I'm not saying those things don't make me happy anymore—they still do. They carried me for thirteen years, through grief, transition, and growth. But lately, I've found joy in a different rhythm—one that asks less of the world and more of myself. *I'm learning that peace can be loud enough to fill a room.*

If you ask me today, my answer is completely different: spending time with myself. Indoors. Creating things I'm passionate about.

Sometimes that looks like writing. Sometimes it's silence. Sometimes it's doing absolutely nothing and letting that be enough.

These days, happiness looks simpler: *resting in my bed, spending quiet hours with myself, creating things I'm passionate about, breathing in the quiet and letting it hold me.*

It might change again. Maybe in six months I'll crave the gym and the restaurants again. Maybe this is just a season of turning inward before I turn outward again.

But right now, this is where I am—still, grounded, grateful. And I'm learning to honour that instead of fighting it.

Lessons From the Quiet Storm

Surviving is not the same as living.

Aftershocks can weigh as much as earthquakes.

Drive can die with the person who inspired it.

Rebuilding takes patience I don't always have.

Self-care isn't always flights or shopping or sweat. Sometimes it's silence, therapy, rest, and saying no.

Success without passion is hollow. Passion without community cannot last.

Grief isn't a subject you finish. It's a curriculum that shifts as you do.

Small Steps Towards Tomorrow

"Discipline is faith in motion."

I name the fear: that this paralysis will steal another decade.

But I know this too: my reconstruction is already faster than my collapse.

The podcast.

The Kit.

This book.

They are proof I am still moving.

So I stop waiting for fire. I choose discipline. Thirty minutes a day. A paragraph. A walk. A call. Small steps that matter more than waiting for lightning.

I am learning to forgive myself for skipping the gym, to stop performing *"fine"* for others, to allow myself to be tired, to relax, and to just chill without plans or goals. I am learning to put myself first, to be unapologetically selfish when it matters, and to reach for community instead of retreating into silence.

I approach counselling as guidance in this new classroom—a tool, not a test of strength or weakness.

Because I am no longer a freshman. I am a graduate of the storm. Now I am enrolled in a harder, quieter course: *learning how to live.*

Class is in session.
And this time, *I'm not skipping. I'm showing up for myself—fully, gently, and on purpose.*

When the Aftershocks Hit

"Naming it is how the shaking stops."

When I felt stuck, I learned that naming it was the first step to movement. Just saying out loud *"I feel paralysed"* gave the feeling less power over me.

When the timeline haunted me (*Why did I waste ten years? Will I waste another ten?*) I had to learn to release it. My healing doesn't match anyone's schedule, not even my own past self's expectations.

When external self-care stopped working, I had to ask what my body actually needed. The answer surprised me: rest, not more activity. Silence, not more stimulation.

When motivation disappeared, I chose discipline instead. I watered the garden of my life a little each day—one conversation, one sentence, one quiet moment of focus, one deep breath, one step forward, one decision to keep going. Slowly, the roots held.

When isolation tempted me, I reminded myself: phase two requires different tools than phase one. Survival mode needed constant motion. Living mode needs community, even when reaching out feels impossible.

Naming What's Next

I had to ask myself some hard questions:

What parts of me are still frozen at twenty-two, the age I was when she died?

How has performing strength for thirteen years drained me completely?

What would inner self-care look like, beyond the comforts and distractions that used to work?

If I feel paralysed, what's one small step I could take today, without needing to see the whole road ahead?

What did I once love that no longer fulfils me? And what new thing is quietly calling?

I don't have all the answers yet. But asking the questions is the work.

For You, If You're Past Crisis But Still Drifting

What parts of you feel frozen at a younger age, and how is that showing up in your life now?

When did you last feel truly alive—not just busy, but purposeful? What's changed since then?

What does self-care actually look like for you now, beyond what used to work years ago?

What questions are you avoiding that might need asking?

Are you surviving or living? How can you tell the difference?

When did external success stop feeling like enough? What does "*enough*" mean to you now?

The Continuing Work

"Survival was the first decade. The second is learning how to live. They are not the same task, and that is why you feel lost again. You are not failing—you are advancing. The lessons are harder now because you've already mastered survival. This is the brutal, beautiful work of living."

Chapter Eighteen

The Bridge

"Grief doesn't end, but neither does love—and this book became the bridge between them."

No Finish Line

"There is no finish line in grief, only new ways to keep walking."

If you carry grief, you already know this: there is no finish line. No clean moment where you *"get over it"* and return to the person you were before.

Grief doesn't end. It changes shape. It settles into your bones, becomes part of the landscape of your daily life. Some days it whispers. Some days it roars. But always, it stays tethered to love.

I lost my mum at twenty-two. More than a decade later, I still find myself reaching for her: in milestones she should have seen, in birthdays she'll never celebrate, in the quiet mornings when her absence is louder than any sound in the room.

You may never stop missing them. I hope you never do. That missing is proof: the love was real, the bond mattered, their presence carved a space nothing else can fill.

But love doesn't vanish with presence. It travels forward. It steadies you in the hardest moments. It shapes who you are becoming. It guides your choices even when the voice is no longer there to answer back.

Grief is a lifelong companion. But so is love. They walk together, inseparable, each one giving the other meaning.

How This Became a Bridge

This book was born from the loneliness of early grief. From the desperate wish that someone would sit beside me in the dark hours and say: *"You are not strange. You are not broken. What you're feeling is not weakness. It is love with nowhere to go."*

It grew from years of learning that survival itself is an act of courage. That showing up each day, even whilst carrying invisible weight, is heroic in ways the world rarely sees.

It became a bridge between who I was before 7 July, 2012, and who I had to become after. A bridge between silence and words. Between my grief and yours. Proof that even in our loneliest moments, we are not as alone as we think.

I am not the same twenty-two-year-old who dropped to her knees on the bathroom floor that day. She was defined by shock. The woman writing these words is defined by endurance—by survival—by the truth that this work was never about erasing my mother's absence, but about building a life wide enough to hold her memory alongside my own survival. And if you're reading this, I hope you build something wide enough too—a life that can hold your loss without being consumed by it. If you've known that kind of breaking, may you also know what it means to keep going—to live, and still carry love within the ache. And if you're somewhere in your own survival, I hope these words remind you that you're not alone in it.

When Creation Became My Anchor

"Creation didn't heal me; it held me steady."

The podcast came first. The first episode was a glimpse into my own story—losing my mum—though never in the depth you'll find in these pages. What followed were eight episodes of other people's grief stories, each one teaching me something about the universality of loss. I invited a psychotherapist and a counsellor onto the podcast to help us digest our grief and answer the questions that often go unspoken. Then came friends who'd lost two friends suddenly to a drunk driver, a mother to illness, a father to COVID, a sibling to suicide—even a child to stillbirth. Each conversation became its own kind of healing.

The tenth episode was meant to be me and my brothers finally talking about our mum together. We tried. I broke down so completely that we couldn't finish filming. Maybe one day we'll try again. Maybe we won't. Both are okay.

The podcast hasn't become financially successful yet—I only launched it early this year, but it was an investment in myself. It gave me purpose when I had none. It reminded me I could still create, still connect, still build something meaningful from the wreckage.

The *SayItKit* grew from the same soil. From regret. From the danger of love left unsaid. I'm still working on it, planning to launch soon. It exists so others might speak now instead of later—so fewer people have to carry the unbearable weight of unspoken words.

And this book—the thing I'm writing now, and will keep shaping while on my solo trip, is my attempt to make sense of thirteen years of surviving and finally learning to live.

All of it (the book, the Kit, the conversations with strangers who say, "*This is what I needed*") emerged from grief, not in spite of it. It was never about closure. It was about making something alive from love that had nowhere else to go.

These projects aren't distractions. They're proof. Proof that something inside me is still alive, still reaching, still choosing to build from broken pieces.

Where I Am Now—October 2025

I work from home, which gives me the freedom I've always craved over stability. My days are quiet—client work, writing, creating, breathing through the hours as they come.

I'm in a season of saying *no*.
No to conversations I don't want to have.
No to plans that cost more energy than they give.
No to performing "fine" for people who haven't earned my truth.

I only have time for the friends who stayed—the ones who held me when I lost my mum. Not out of resentment, but protection. My love tank is still refilling, slowly, carefully, learning how to pour without emptying myself for people who can't hold it gently.

I used to expect everyone to love like I love—fiercely, attentively, remembering the small things. Grief taught me that not everyone speaks the same language of care. Not everyone can give what I give. And that's okay. I meet people where they meet me now.

I still live with a flatmate, though he's rarely home—most days, it feels like my own quiet sanctuary. For a long time, silence terrified me. Now, the hum of the street outside helps me breathe through the stillness. Some nights are calm. Others are harder—the kind that stir old panic, where a story or a headline can pull me back into memory. But I stay. I no longer run from the noise inside me. I fight through it, inch by inch, until the ache softens enough to let me rest.

That's progress. Thirteen years ago, I couldn't sleep without someone in the next room. For years, being alone felt like terror. Now, even with the echoes that return, I can stay in my own space. I can face the night.

And even that—imperfect as it is—matters.

What I'm Looking Forward To

"Hope is a small light, but it travels far."

Solo travel—lots of it. Healing retreats. Yoga. Meditation. Long mornings with my journal and the kind of stillness that doesn't ask for permission. Finding ways to turn my passions into purpose, without hustling myself into exhaustion.

I used to say I wanted to grow old with good friends more than I wanted romantic love. My mum's presence was so powerful that it shaped the way I saw women—as anchors, protectors, sacred companions. I've always held female friendship as holy ground.

But this season is teaching me something new.
I am more whole in my own company than I ever realised.
I don't need constant conversation to feel connected.
I don't need to fill silence to feel alive.
I can just be—and that, too, is a kind of love.

Life is too short to work yourself numb.
Too short to measure worth by productivity.
Too fragile to spend it proving your value to people who can't see it.

"Positive vibes" isn't a caption for me—it's survival. A way of honouring the days my mum's body couldn't carry the weight of everything she gave. A promise to myself that I'll never mistake burnout for purpose again.

I'm learning to live gently, to move slowly, to breathe deeply.

To build a life that doesn't rush me through my own peace.

Starting Therapy Again

I was meant to start therapy again before the year ended. November, maybe. But life had other plans. Another loss touched my circle, and grief came rushing back through the cracks I thought had healed. The panic returned. The sleeplessness. The reminders that healing isn't linear—that someone else's pain can still awaken your own.

So therapy will begin next year instead. And that's okay.

The first round of therapy was about survival—panic attacks, anxiety, the chaos of early grief. That work saved my life. This round will be about something deeper. The quiet battle between old me and new me. The go-getter who died with my mum, and the version trying to resurface now.

It will be about learning how to want again—to want success without fearing it, to want rest without guilt, to want life without waiting for loss to follow.

It will be about remembering who I am in this second season. Because I'm still lost. Still figuring it out. Still learning what to keep and what to let go of.

But at least now I know being lost isn't failure.
At least now I have tools.
At least now I'm not drowning.

What Love Built After Loss

"Love rebuilds what grief tried to destroy."

If you're reading this book, here's what I've discovered:

I still cry. I still have days that sink into sadness, confusion, and the quiet ache of missing my mum. I still have moments where the world feels too heavy, and others where it feels impossibly light. Grief hasn't changed in that way.

But I've learned to live with it.

Grief became my companion—an uninvited guest who never left, but slowly learned how to share the space. Some days we sit quietly beside each other. Other days, it storms through me until I can barely breathe. Yet, even in that chaos, I've learned: it's all part of living.

There are loud moments and silent ones.
Days that undo me and days that rebuild me.
Both belong. Both are normal.

As long as I'm not hurting myself, as long as I reach out when I need help, I'm doing fine. Even when I'm crying, withdrawn, or lost for words—I'm still okay. Because surviving, in whatever shape it takes, is still surviving.

Thirteen years later, I'm walking proof.
Still broken in places. Still learning. Still unsure.
But also—deeply alive.
I understand my pain now. I welcome it, even, because it's my way of staying connected to my mum.

I've learned that grief isn't the opposite of joy—it's a doorway to it. The heart that can break that deeply is also capable of loving that deeply. And that kind of love doesn't vanish; it just changes form.

For You, If You're Ready to Build Something

Are you letting yourself feel what you need to feel?

Are you being as gentle with yourself as you deserve?

What small thing could you start building now, even if it feels too modest for your grief?

If love were a verb today, what would it have you make, tend, or continue?

When the Heaviness Returns

When the nights stretched long, when anniversaries stung, when I wondered if I'd ever feel whole again—I had to remember: grief walks with me always, but so does love. I learned to let one steady the other.

When the heaviness returned, I tried to welcome it. It was my mum's impact echoing through my body—a reminder that love can still make itself known through ache. I'd tell myself: *this ache exists because she existed.*

Then I'd pause.
Sit with it.
Let the silence hold me.

I discovered I was never truly alone.
Even in the quiet, even in the weight of missing her—love is here too. Changed. Reshaped. But unbreakable.

Always a companion.
Always a bridge.
Always proof that what matters most never really leaves.

A Letter to the Girl I Was

"If I could go back, I'd tell her: you'll survive this."

If I could go back to that bathroom, to that hospital corridor, to the girl who thought her life was ending, here's what I'd say:

You will be okay.

Not in the way you think "okay" means right now. Not the kind of okay where the pain stops or the absence fills—but the kind where you learn to breathe around it. Where you build a life big enough to hold both the love and the loss.

It's okay not to be okay. The song *It's OK* by Nightbirde says this better than I ever could. Sometimes I listen with tears slipping down my face—not in despair, but in release. I've mentioned her music before in my rituals, and it still helps; a reminder that we are forever rediscovering ourselves, meeting new versions of who we are—confused, lost, found, and lost again.

Right now, when you feel like you're not okay, you're actually more okay than you realise. You're surviving. And survival is the work. Everything else is extra.

Grief will teach you things you never wanted to learn. It will reshape you in ways you'll resist. But it will also make you more compassionate, more present, more aware of what truly matters.

And one day, you'll write a book about all of this. You'll create tools to help others. You'll turn the worst thing that ever happened to you into something that makes people feel less alone.

That doesn't make losing her worth it—nothing ever could. But it means her love didn't die with her. It just changed form. It lives in you now. And you get to decide what to do with it.

How I Carry Love Forward

There's a quiet ritual that travels with me—the soft glow of a candle, its scent curling through the air, the warmth reminding me that love still lives in the simplest of things. Sometimes, as the flame flickers, I speak to her softly—*Mum, I miss you. Mum, I'm still here—still finding my way.* Her love stays, quiet and steady, like light that refuses to dim.

Anniversaries no longer feel like obligations; they've become gentle pauses for remembrance, not pressure. I honour her quietly, in ways that feel true—through laughter, stillness, scent, and song—without the weight of expectation.

And when the ache feels unbearable, I return to this truth: *Grief is the shadow of love, and shadows only exist because light is real.*

The Continuing Story

"There is no ending here—only another beginning shaped by love."

This is not the end of your story. It's the beginning of a new chapter—one where love takes on new forms, where memory becomes medicine, where grief transforms from weight into wisdom.

You carry their love forward now.
Not because you've healed,
but because you're still here.

And being here is enough.
That's all survival ever asked of me—to still be here.

Some days I do it well.

Some days I barely do it at all.
But every single day, I'm still here.
Still breathing.
Still carrying her forward.

And if you're reading this, so are you.
That matters more than you know.

And Somehow, Enough

Grief carves out a space in us. What we choose to fill that space with becomes the measure of our survival. I chose love. I chose memory. I chose to keep building, even when the foundation felt shattered. And somehow, that was enough.

Chapter Nineteen

Reclaiming Myself—The Work in Progress

"We are not lost in grief; we are learning to walk in a new light, one step at a time."

Grief changes everything. It reshapes the way I move, the way I think, the way I inhabit my own body. It carves quiet hollows inside me I didn't know existed, leaving echoes in moments both ordinary and monumental. And yet, in that space, a pulse of me waits to be remembered. Not the me I was, not the me the world expects, but the me quietly calling myself back, reclaiming my own presence and remembering who I am.

This chapter is messy, real, sometimes exhausting, but it is necessary. It is the chapter of what I am learning, what I am working on, and the questions I am living with. It is a chapter of living in the unknown, and slowly, courageously, letting pieces of myself come back into view.

The Woman in the Mirror

"Rediscovery begins when you stop rushing your own becoming."

Some mornings I wake and feel a hollow echo of who I used to be. My mind is crowded with questions that have no easy answers. I ask myself: who am I, beyond the roles I hold, the projects I lead, the personas I perform? Which parts of me have I silenced to be accepted, to feel safe, to keep moving forward? How do I honour my grief without letting it define me, without letting it trap me in memory?

I'm learning to meet myself with softness, practising the art of slowing down without guilt. I want to leap forward, create, heal, feel fully alive; yet sometimes the grief whispers that I am not ready, that the world is too loud, that I am still too raw. In those moments, I am learning to breathe, to simply be, and to recognise that this hesitation is not failure but part of the process. Rediscovery is not linear. Healing is not linear.

For You, If You're Learning to See Yourself Again

How do you sit with the parts of yourself that feel paused or unfinished?

When your questions feel heavy, how will you hold yourself with care?

The Questions Guiding My Days

"Asking is its own kind of healing."

I am sitting with questions that feel larger than any single answer. These are the questions I carry with me through mornings, evenings, and quiet pockets of the day:

If I could not define myself by what I do, what words would describe me?

When I am truly alone, what feels like home inside me?

What do I need emotionally, spiritually, and mentally that no one else can give me?

What parts of myself have I been shrinking, silencing, or hiding from the world?

If fear dissolved tomorrow, what would I do differently?

When I imagine my highest self, how do they move through life daily?

Sometimes I feel fleeting clarity. Other times, I feel entirely lost. But I am learning that the act of asking, of living in these questions, is itself reclamation.

The Questions That Still Whisper Back

"The questions you avoid often hold the answers you need most."

Who are you? If you could describe yourself without using your roles (mother, sister, friend, entrepreneur) what words would you choose? If you could describe yourself beyond your titles and obligations, what would you say?

What qualities or feelings do you want people to feel after they've been with you?

Imagine losing all titles, money, status, followers, even your projects. What parts of you would remain intact?

What are the things you'd still choose to do even if you never got credit or validation?

What parts of yourself have you been avoiding meeting, afraid to recognise, or hesitant to nurture?

When do you feel most yourself, not just happy or productive, but deeply alive?

What values or principles would you still hold even if no one approved?

What questions keep you awake at night, and how do you sit with them?

For You, If You're Carrying Big Questions

Which questions are you carrying quietly, perhaps afraid of answering, yet longing to name?

What would it feel like to meet them without judgement?

Lessons in Becoming

"Becoming is remembering what has always been true."

Listening to my own voice, my own body, my own heart—this is where healing begins. Joy can exist in fragments, tucked into small moments: the warmth of sunlight on my skin, the echo of a meaningful conversation, the quiet satisfaction of creating something that matters.

My value is not in what I produce or how I serve others, but in presence—showing up for myself, witnessing my own process, allowing space for tenderness. Contradictions are okay: I can be grieving and hopeful, strong and tender, ambitious and content. Life after grief is not about "moving on", but about integrating the loss into a fuller, more conscious version of myself.

I notice patterns now—what excites me, what drains me, what feels like reclaiming energy rather than losing it. I recognise my values more clearly: authenticity, compassion, curiosity, emotional honesty. These are my compass, guiding me quietly through moments of uncertainty.

For You, If You're Softening After Strength

What patterns are emerging in your life now?

Which values feel most alive to you, and where do you notice them in your day?

Learning to Return to Myself

"Coming home to yourself takes time—and tenderness."

Reclaiming myself is slower than I thought it would be. It is not a checklist, not a finish line. It is in the small choices: choosing words that matter, creating spaces that heal, honouring boundaries, listening to what I truly need rather than what is expected of me.

I ask myself questions often, not as instructions to follow but as mirrors to see what is alive inside me:

What am I ready to step fully into now?

Which old stories am I ready to release?

How can I show up for myself today in a way my past self could only dream of?

Sometimes it is monumental. Sometimes it is simply noticing that I am breathing, that I am here, that I am still me, even if changed. I am learning that reclaiming myself is about embracing the paradoxes, the contradictions, the moments of grief and moments of joy, and seeing that they can coexist.

Learning to Trust What's Working

"Progress doesn't need perfection to be real."

Life reminds me of the power of focusing on what actually works instead of stressing over what I can't control. I began developing my SayItKit before deciding to formally create this book, and while it's taking longer to launch than I expected, the book is moving forward and giving me more momentum and clarity. This is a reminder that progress doesn't always follow the order we plan, and presence often brings results in ways we can't predict.

For You, If You're Ready to Begin Again

Which parts of yourself are you ready to reclaim?

Which small steps can you focus on that actually work right now?

The Courage of Saying No

"Saying no is not rejection; it's respect for your own capacity."

For years, I said yes when I meant no. I made excuses instead of being honest. *"Something came up." "I have an event." "I'm not available."* All polite lies to avoid admitting the truth: I didn't have the energy, the capacity, or the desire to show up.

I thought protecting other people's feelings was more important than protecting my own peace. So I performed availability I didn't feel, drained my already empty love tank, and resented myself for it afterwards.

Reclaiming myself has meant learning to tell the truth, even when it's uncomfortable.

Now, when a friend calls and I'm not in the right headspace, I don't pick up. When someone asks to meet and I don't have the emotional bandwidth, I say it plainly: *"Right now, I'm not in the best place to socialise. I'm sorry."*

No elaborate excuses. No performance of busyness. Just honesty.

It feels vulnerable every time. Part of me still worries they'll think I don't care, that I'm selfish, that I'm a bad friend. But the truth is this: I don't call my friends when I'm in crisis. I reach out after I've climbed out of the darkness myself. So when I'm in the thick of it, when my love tank is bone-dry, I cannot pour into anyone else.

Saying no isn't cruelty. It's self-preservation. It's choosing myself when no one else can choose me. And that is reclamation.

For You, If You're Reclaiming Your Voice

Where have you been performing availability you don't feel?

What would it look like to say no honestly, without guilt or justification?

The Work in Progress

"You are allowed to be unfinished and still worthy of love."

I am not finished. I am raw. I am learning. Perhaps that is exactly where I need to be. Every question I carry, every reflection I sit with, every small joy I allow myself to feel, is part of the reclamation.

I am learning that it is okay to be a work in progress—that life, identity, and selfhood are not destinations but ongoing acts of presence, courage, and attention.

I am asking, I am listening, I am noticing, and I am reclaiming.

For You, If You're Still Figuring It Out

How do you notice yourself growing in the quiet moments?

What does being a work in progress feel like for you right now?

Reflections on Reclamation

"Reclamation is not arrival; it's the courage to begin again."

Reclamation is not a destination; it is living in the questions and daring to answer them honestly.

It is the quiet commitment to begin again—every day, in small ways.

It is allowing yourself to become who you already are, without rushing the unfolding.

Chapter Twenty

Thirteen Years Later: The Life Grief Built

"Grief doesn't end. But neither does the person I'm becoming because of it."

I used to think grief had an endpoint. That if I worked hard enough, cried long enough, processed deeply enough, I would eventually arrive at a place called "*healed*." A destination where the pain would soften into something manageable, where I could say with confidence: *I'm okay now.*

But I know the truth now. There is no destination. Grief is not a problem to solve or a wound that fully closes. It is the shape my love takes now that my mum is gone. And that shape will keep shifting for the rest of my life.

This final chapter is not about offering you a neat conclusion or a blueprint for "moving on." It is about sharing what grief has taught me after more than a decade of living alongside it. Some of these lessons came early. Others are still revealing themselves, year after year, as I continue to evolve and grief evolves with me.

If you are holding this book because you are grieving, know this: what I've learned may not match what you will learn. Grief is as individual as fingerprints. But perhaps in my reflections, you will find echoes of your own truth.

The Depth of Love, The Weight of Loss

"How deeply you grieve is how deeply you loved."

One of the most important things I've learned is this: the intensity of your grief mirrors the intensity of how you feel everything else in life.

I am an empath. I feel deeply, love fiercely, connect intensely. I pour myself into relationships, wear my heart openly, and live with my emotions close to the surface. This is not weakness. It is simply how I am wired.

When my mum died, grief hit me like a tidal wave because that is how I experience everything. My panic attacks weren't just anxiety. They were my body screaming the loss I couldn't yet put into words. My sleepless nights weren't just insomnia. They were love with nowhere to land, circling endlessly in the dark.

For someone like me, someone who feels everything at full volume, grief becomes an all-consuming force. It doesn't visit politely. It moves in, rearranges the furniture, and refuses to leave. And for years, I thought that meant I was broken. That something was wrong with me for feeling it so intensely whilst others seemed to *"handle it better."*

But I've learned this isn't true. There is no *"better"* or *"worse"* way to grieve. There is only your way.

If you are someone who feels deeply, your grief will be deep. If you love with your whole heart, losing someone will crack that heart wide open. And that is not a flaw. That is proof of how fully you lived and loved whilst they were here.

On the other hand, if you are someone who processes emotions more quietly, who keeps feelings private, who moves through life with a steadier, less turbulent emotional rhythm, your grief may look entirely different. It may be subtle. It may be internal. You may not cry in public or talk about your loss openly. And that is equally valid.

Grief does not measure worth by tears shed or words spoken. It simply reflects the way you are built to feel.

And however you feel it, you are doing it right.

Grief as Fuel, Grief as Weight

"Grief moves through each of us differently—none of it is wrong."

One of the most misunderstood truths about grief is this: it does not affect everyone the same way, even when they have lost the same person.

Some people channel grief into momentum. It becomes their fuel, their drive, their reason to push forward. They work harder, achieve more, build empires in honour of the person they lost. Grief propels them forward like wind in their sails.

For others, grief does the opposite. It becomes a weight so heavy that even getting out of bed feels like a victory; ambition fades, motivation disappears, and the fire that once burned bright flickers and dims. Grief does not push them forward. It anchors them in place, and every step requires monumental effort.

Neither response is better. Neither is more *"correct."* They are simply different ways that grief moves through different people.

For me, grief was never fuel—it was weight. Grief did not make me stronger, more driven, or more ambitious. It depleted me. It stole my fire and left me struggling to find even a spark.

Before my mum died, I was unstoppable—driven, full of plans and dreams, and unshakeable in my confidence. When she died, all of that died too. For years, I watched other people channel their grief into achievement whilst I could barely function. I judged myself harshly for it. *Why can't I be like them? Why am I not turning this pain into purpose? Why does grief make me weaker instead of stronger?*

But grief moves differently in everyone.

I see it in people like my friend Hauwa—the ones who somehow turn pain into power.

We met back in 2015 at the airport in Lagos, both on the same flight to the United States for a documentary filmmaking workshop at Montana State University. We were part of a scholarship-sponsored programme, living and studying together for a few months—an experience that quietly shaped how we each saw the world.

Over time, our friendship grew into something deeply grounding. She's one of those quiet forces—steady, focused, resilient in a way that both amazes and humbles me. I've watched her walk through loss with a kind of strength that doesn't shout; it simply endures.

She lost her mum, and later her dad too, and somehow found a way to keep building, to keep showing up for life. Born and raised in Nigeria, she carries that quietly determined mindset of *"life must continue."*

Her grief doesn't paralyse her when it comes to her work or her drive—perhaps it does in ways I've never seen. On reflection, I've never really asked her how her grief affects her. But what I do see is how it sharpens her focus.

She works, she achieves, she builds.

It's as if loss became her fuel, propelling her forward with purpose and grace. When I watch her, I see someone who transforms loss into momentum, someone who channels pain into drive and direction. This is something I truly admire about her. It is not easy, and it feels like a remarkable skill—a way of carrying loss that turns pain into purpose.

Years ago, we had a moment where our different grief styles were misunderstood. I withdrew for a while. But recently, when I spent time with her in Nigeria, we spoke openly about how differently we each process loss. That conversation drew us closer, and through it, I realised something simple and freeing:

we grieve differently, and that's okay.

Understanding how differently we grieve has taught me something essential: there is no right way. Her way isn't better than mine. Mine isn't better than hers. We simply carry the same loss in different vessels.

And that's the truth about grief—it never wears the same face twice. The way it moves through one person may look nothing like how it moves through another. What feels like fuel to one might feel like weight to someone else.

Deby experiences grief differently. When I once told her about going through my darkest moments, she said, *"Oh no, no, no. I don't go through darkness."* And I realised we are built differently. What overwhelms me might not overwhelm her—not because she doesn't grieve, but perhaps her mind and heart process loss in a way that does not engulf her. Her sisters, however, grieve more like I do: as a weight that makes everything harder, a presence that cannot be ignored.

With quiet concern, Deby sometimes says, *"eloho, maybe talk to my sisters—I think you understand their kind of grief."*

Even within the same family, even after losing the same people, grief speaks different languages.

I've also had friends tell me, *"Don't let it consume you,"* as if grief is a choice I can simply refuse. As if I'm passively allowing it to take over, when the truth is I am fighting every single day just to keep my head above water.

Those words, though well-meaning, come from people who experience grief differently. For them, grief is something they manage—something they move through without being paralysed by it. They genuinely believe that if I just tried harder, stayed busier, adopted a different mindset, I could *"overcome"* it the way they have.

But that's not how grief works for me. It's not something I choose or control—I've tried. Again and again. Yet it moves through me on its own terms. My entire existence has been about learning to live alongside it, not forcing it into meaning or achievement.

There is nothing beautiful about losing my mum. Nothing. I cannot spin it into a positive narrative. I cannot say *"grief made me better" or "I'm grateful for what it taught me."* Those words feel like lies in my mouth.

What I lost was irreplaceable. What I carry is unbearable some days. And the fact that I am still here, still breathing, still trying, is not because grief made me stronger—it is because I refused to let it kill me, even when it tried.

This is where temperament matters. The way you naturally move through life shapes how grief moves through you.

I am soft, tender, affectionate, deeply emotional. I feel everything at full volume. I love with my whole heart, cry easily, connect intensely. That is who I am, and it is beautiful. But it also means that when loss came, it shattered me completely.

People who are naturally less emotional, who process feelings more privately, who keep a steadier rhythm through life, may experience grief differently. It may not consume them the way it consumes me. Not because they loved less, but because their emotional wiring is different.

This is what I need people to understand: if grief has become your fuel, I am genuinely happy for you. I admire your ability to channel pain into purpose, to build something meaningful from the wreckage. That is a gift, and it is valid.

But if grief has become your weight—if it has drained you, slowed you down, stolen your ambition, and left you struggling just to survive—that is also valid. You are not failing. You are not weak. You are not "*letting*" grief win.

You are simply carrying a different kind of load. And the fact that you are still here, still trying, still breathing, is proof of your strength—even if it doesn't look like achievement to the outside world.

Some people grieve positively. Some people grieve quietly. Most of us grieve somewhere in between—in a messy, contradictory mix of both.

All of it is okay. All of it is real. All of it deserves to be honoured without judgement.

If you are someone who has channelled grief into fuel, I see you. Keep building. Keep moving. Keep honouring them through your work.

And if you are someone who is drowning in the weight, I see you too. Keep breathing. Keep surviving. Keep showing up, even when it feels impossible.

Both are grief. Both are love. And both, in their own way, are enough.

The Seasons That Return

"Grief doesn't pass through time; it circles it."

In the beginning, I believed grief followed a path—denial, anger, bargaining, depression, acceptance.
I thought if I could just work through each stage methodically, I would eventually graduate to the final one and be done.

But grief is not a staircase you climb.
It is a spiral you walk again and again—visiting the same emotions at different depths each time you circle back.

Some years, anger returned, and I raged at my mum for leaving me too soon.

Other years, I felt nothing but numbness, moving through life like a ghost in my own body.

There were seasons where I believed I had finally made peace with her absence, only to be blindsided by a grief wave so powerful it felt like day one all over again.

This is normal.

This is how grief works.
You will not "get over it."
You will learn to carry it.
And some days that weight will feel lighter.
Other days, it will crush you.
Both are part of the same process.

The second season of grief—the one I'm living in now, thirteen years later—has taught me that loss doesn't fade with time. It simply becomes part of your landscape.
You learn to navigate around it.
You build your life alongside it.
But it never disappears.

And that's okay.
Missing her is not a problem to solve.
It is proof that she mattered.
That she still matters.

Each return is softer now—less like drowning, more like remembering.
Grief changes its temperature, but never its truth.
It circles back not to break me, but to remind me: love is still here.

Grief and the Shape of Me Now

"Loss reshapes us, but it doesn't erase us."

Before my mum died, I knew exactly who I was. Ambitious, driven, unstoppable. I had plans, dreams, a clear vision of the life I was building.

When she died, that version of me died too.

For years, I mourned two losses: her, and the version of myself that vanished with her. I didn't recognise the person I'd become. My priorities shifted. My values changed. The things that once seemed vital—success, recognition, achievement—now felt hollow, stripped of meaning.

I thought I was broken—that grief had stolen my identity and left me with nothing.

But slowly, I began to see it differently. Grief hadn't destroyed me; it had reshaped me. And the person I was becoming wasn't weaker or lesser than the one I'd been—just changed.

This is one of grief's cruelest truths: it asks you to rebuild yourself from the ground up while still carrying the weight of what you've lost. You are not the same person you were before—you can't be. Loss alters you at a cellular level.

But within that truth, there is mercy: you get to choose who you become next.

I am no longer the girl who once chased recognition and perfection. I am a woman who values peace, rest, meaningful connection, and the courage to speak about what hurts. I am someone who understands that life is fragile, that time is never promised, and that love is the only thing worth carrying forward.

Grief reshaped me—but it did not break me.
And it will not break you either.

Grief Has Its Own Clock

"You can't rush what moves by its own rhythm."

This is perhaps the hardest lesson: you don't get to choose when grief visits, how long it stays, or what shape it takes.

You can be fine for months—living your life, feeling steady—and then a song plays on the radio, or a familiar scent drifts through the air, and suddenly you are on your knees in the middle of a grocery store, sobbing into your hands whilst strangers pretend not to notice.

You can't predict the triggers. You can't schedule the breakdowns. You can't force yourself to *"get over it"* by sheer willpower.

Grief moves to its own rhythm, keeping time with a clock you cannot see. And the only way to survive it is to stop trying to fight its timing.

I spent years trying to outrun my grief. I moved countries. I filled my days with distractions. I convinced myself that if I just stayed busy enough, strong enough, productive enough, the pain would eventually give up and leave me alone.

It didn't work. Grief is patient. It will wait. And when you finally stop running, it will still be there—ready to be felt.

Even in the smallest moments—showering, walking, scrolling through social media, or sitting with someone who casually mentions their family—you may feel its presence. Tears may come, not from sadness, but from quiet recognition. In those moments, grief becomes a beautiful ache—a reminder of how deeply you loved.

The only way through is through. Not around. Not over. *Through.*

That means allowing yourself to cry when the tears come. To retreat when you need solitude. To feel anger without guilt, sadness without shame, and numbness without judgement.

It means granting yourself permission to grieve in whatever way your body and heart need—even if it doesn't look like anyone else's version of healing.

You are not failing if you're still grieving years later.
You are simply still loving.
And love does not expire.

The Loneliness Within Love

"Even when love surrounds you, grief reminds you what only you can carry."

One of the most isolating aspects of grief is this: even when surrounded by people who care, you can feel utterly alone.

Because no one else lost your relationship with them. No one else carries your specific memories. No one else knows the private jokes, the late-night conversations, the small moments that only you shared.

My brothers lost our mum. But they did not lose *my mum*—the woman who was my everything, my protector, my mirror. That loss is mine alone to carry.

This is why grief can feel so lonely even in a room full of people who love you. Because no matter how much they care, they cannot fully understand the exact shape of your loss.

And that is okay. You are not asking them to carry it for you. You are simply asking them to sit beside you whilst you carry it yourself.

The people who stayed in my life were not the ones who had perfect words or solutions. They were the ones who showed up consistently, who didn't disappear when my grief became inconvenient, who let me be broken without trying to fix me.

If you are grieving, surround yourself with people who can hold space for your pain without needing to erase it.

And if you are supporting someone who is grieving, know this: your presence matters more than your words.
Just stay.

When Pain Learns to Whisper

"What was once chaos becomes a quieter kind of love."

I thought grief would plateau. That after the first few brutal years, I would reach a steady state and stay there.

But grief is not static. It evolves. Every year, I discover new layers of loss I hadn't yet touched.

In the first year, I grieved her physical absence. The sound of her voice. The warmth of her hugs. The everyday rituals we shared.

In the second and third years, I grieved the future we would never have. The milestones she would miss. The conversations we would never finish.

In the years that followed, I began to grieve the person I might have been if she had lived—the version of me who would have had her guidance through my twenties and thirties. The daughter who would have called her for advice, celebrated victories with her, shared ordinary moments of life.

Now, thirteen years later, I grieve new things: the comfort of a message from my mum just asking how I'm doing, or a quick phone call to say, *Mum, what do you think of this?*

I even miss her fussing over me in that way only mothers can—the kind of care that once felt a little annoying but now feels precious.

I often think about how, as I've grown older, it would have been my turn to look after her, to pamper her, to return the love and gentleness she gave me.

I also grieve the moments that might have been—more laughter, family trips, more fun with my brothers and nieces, the kind of simple, joyful memories that would have kept her presence alive between us.

And the sister I never had but desperately needed after she died.

In the early years, grief was a scream—raw, wild, unrelenting. It dragged me six feet under and called that place home. It was an overdose of emotion I couldn't come down from—no air, no balance, no sense of time. Just the weight. Just the darkness. But with time, something shifted. The pain didn't vanish; it *mutated.* It learned a new language. What was once unbearable became strangely familiar—almost tender. The ache began to hum instead of howl. It still visits, but now it knocks softly. It doesn't destroy; it reminds.

It no longer feels like dying. It feels like remembering. Like love that refuses to leave—quiet, constant, alive in its own way. What was once chaos is now a strange kind of beauty—*a pain that breathes.*

Each layer reveals itself when I am ready. Not before. Not on anyone else's schedule.

This is what living with grief means: you do not *"get over it"* and move on. You integrate it. You learn to hold both the love and the loss at the same time.

And as you grow and change, your grief grows and changes with you.

You will spend the rest of your life learning new things about what you lost. And that is not a failure.

That is the depth of love made visible.

When Joy Returns, Gently

"Joy is not forgetting—it's remembering with lightness."

For years, I believed that being happy meant I had forgotten her—that joy was a kind of betrayal, a quiet act of disloyalty to her memory.

I punished myself for laughing. I felt guilty when I enjoyed something. I convinced myself that if I wasn't actively suffering, I wasn't properly honouring her.

But grief and joy are not opposites. They are companions—two hands that learn to hold the same heart.

You can miss someone desperately and still find moments of lightness. You can carry loss and still build a life worth living.

Happiness is not disrespect. It is survival. It is proof that love did not die with them. It is choosing to honour their memory by living fully, even though they are gone.

My mum would never have wanted me to spend my life drowning in sorrow. She poured everything into me so I could thrive, not so I could collapse.

Choosing joy is not moving on.

It is moving forward—carefully, consciously, whilst still carrying her with me.

If you are grieving and you catch yourself smiling, don't pull back. Don't apologise.
That smile is not forgetting. It is remembering—remembering that even in its brokenness, life still holds beauty.

The Ache That Never Leaves

"Some aches are forever—not as wounds, but as witnesses."

I will never stop wishing she were here.
I will never stop imagining what life would look like if she hadn't died.
I will never stop feeling the ache when I see mothers and daughters together —
when someone casually mentions calling their mum,
when I realise how many years have passed without her.

Some wounds do not heal. They simply become part of you.
And that is not a sign of failure or weakness.
It is a testament to how much she mattered —
how much she *still* matters.

Grief is love with nowhere to go.
And as long as I love her, I will grieve her.
Not every day with the same intensity.
Not always in the same way.
But *always*.

That is the quiet trade-off for deep love: deep loss.
And I would make that trade again—every single time.

The Then, the Now, the Still

"Healing is not linear; it's a language you keep relearning."

Thirteen years later, people assume the panic has passed.
That time has softened the edges of grief.
That I've *moved* on or *healed* —
or whatever other phrase people use when they don't know what else to say.

The truth is more complicated than that.
Some things have changed.
Some things haven't.

And some things, I'm still learning to live with.

Then

Three months after my mum died, I went to her graveside. That night, lying in bed, something inside me snapped.
My chest tightened. My heart raced. I thought I was going crazy.
I thought I was having a heart attack.

I didn't know what panic attacks were. I didn't know what anxiety meant. I just knew I was dying—and no one could convince me otherwise.

Back then, I couldn't be alone. The darkness terrified me. *Sleep felt like surrender,* like if I closed my eyes, I might not wake up. My mum had died, and suddenly I was convinced death was coming for me too.

And the anger. I was so angry. So bitter. I hated the world.

Just recently, on the drive back from visiting a family friend, my auntie told me I've come a long way. She said I used to be so angry—it was in my face, my mannerisms, my responses to everything. I was shocked.
I said, "Wow, really?"
She said, "Of course."

I thought it was only my friends who experienced that side of me, but apparently everyone saw it. I was furious at life, at God, at the unfairness of it all.

Everything felt dangerous. The world had shown me it could take everything in an instant, and I lived in constant fear that it would happen again.

I stayed at my friend Joy's house in the middle of the night, shaking and breathless, because being alone felt impossible. The thought of it sent me spiralling. I needed someone in the next room—someone whose presence I could feel, someone who could call an ambulance if I stopped breathing.

My friends used to say I kept talking about how "the cloud is dark." I couldn't escape the heaviness. It followed me everywhere.

During the pandemic, when things got really bad, I started meditating. That helped a bit—gave me something to hold on to when the anxiety felt overwhelming.

Now

Thirteen years later, my triggers haven't disappeared—they've just shifted.

Darkness still gets me. Once the sun sets and the world goes quiet, the anxiety creeps in. Being alone still terrifies me. *I don't think I could ever live by myself.* The thought of it makes my chest tighten even now.

During the pandemic, it got worse. The sound of ambulance sirens outside my window would send me into a spiral. Every siren felt like a reminder that death was everywhere—that I wasn't safe, that no one was safe. The isolation, the fear, the constant presence of loss. It brought everything back.

But after the pandemic, when I moved out of Tare's house and started living with flatmates, the anxiety eased. Not completely. But enough.

Having someone else in the flat—even if we didn't speak—made me feel safer. I explained to my flatmates that if I didn't say good morning or hello, it wasn't rudeness. I was recovering: from depression, from sadness, from anxiety, from the paranoia and trauma of isolation. They understood.

For a long time, I was fine. Stable. The panic attacks became rare. I learned how to manage the anxiety—how to recognise when it was creeping in and gently push the thoughts away before they consumed me.

But recently, it came back.

When a family friend lost her husband suddenly, the anxiety returned. Not as severe as before, but still there—the fear, the sleepless nights, the intrusive thoughts whispering that loss is always waiting, always just around the corner.

My flatmate hasn't been home much, so I've been alone more often, and the old familiar terror started knocking at the door again.

I'm more in control now than I was back then. I recognise the signs. I know what helps. I drink magnesium to help me relax and sleep. I live on a high street where I can see people walking outside my window, and that makes me feel safer. *I remind myself that I've survived this before—and I can survive it again.*

But I still hate being alone. I'm learning to sit with that fear instead of running from it. Because the reality is, life will require me to be alone sometimes. And I can't spend the rest of my life terrified of my own company.

Still

Some things don't trigger me anymore.

I can face reminders of her without unravelling.
I don't panic at sudden sounds or passing memories the way I used to.
I can sleep most nights without the overwhelming fear that I won't wake up.

The constant, suffocating terror of those early years has lifted. I'm not drowning anymore. I'm treading water. Some days, I'm even swimming.

But hospitals? I still hate them. I'd rather not visit anyone in a hospital—that would be my worst nightmare. And every time I drive past St Thomas' Hospital, I'm reminded: that's where my mum passed away. That place holds a weight I can't shake.

Being alone still gets me.
Darkness still makes me uneasy.
Conversations about death at night still linger too long.

I've learned to set boundaries. You can ask me these questions in the daytime, but once night falls, I'd rather not talk about it. I know it will stay in my mind, and sleep—my fragile peace—will pay the price.

The biggest difference is this: I know what I'm dealing with now. Back then, I thought I was dying. I thought something was physically wrong with me. Now I know it's anxiety—grief showing up in my body.

And knowing that doesn't make it disappear, but it makes it *bearable*. It makes it *nameable*. It gives shape to what once felt like chaos.

There's power in recognising the storm when it returns—because now, I no longer mistake the thunder for the end of the world.

The Shape of Knowing

"You are not failing by remembering; you are honouring by surviving."

Grief doesn't disappear. It just changes shape.

Thirteen years later, I'm not "healed." I'm not "over it." But I'm also not the person I was at twenty-two, paralysed by fear and convinced I was going to die. I've learned how to live alongside the anxiety instead of being consumed by it.

Some triggers will probably always be there. And that's okay. I don't need to be fearless. I just need to keep going.

If you're years into your grief and still struggling with triggers, with anxiety, with the weight of loss, know this: you're not broken. You're not doing it wrong. Grief doesn't follow a timeline. It doesn't fade neatly with time.

But you do learn to carry it. You learn what helps. You learn how to recognise the signs before the panic takes over. You learn that surviving one day means you can survive the next.

And some days, surviving is everything.

The Act of Continuing

"Continuation is its own kind of courage."

The rituals have changed again.

I've always reached for natural solutions. Recently, I discovered magnesium—it relaxes me without numbing me, feels more like taking vitamin C than masking symptoms with drugs. It helps me sleep without the fear that used to come with closing my eyes.

My living situation has become part of my survival. I'm on the top floor, with two flats below me. Knowing people are beneath me helps. My high street is busy—KFC across the road stays open until 1 or 2 a.m. When I look out my window, I see people walking, cars passing, buses moving, stores still lit up. I can even see into other buildings—other apartments, other lives unfolding. It's not noisy, but the movement reminds me that life continues. Seeing it—hearing it—keeps me grounded in ways I never expected.

My flatmate is rarely home, which has forced me to face what I avoided for thirteen years: being truly alone. Not for a night or a weekend, but for months at a time.
And here's the shift—*I'm not just surviving it. I'm choosing it.*

I've always enjoyed spending time with myself. I could take a month to recharge, retreat into my own space, and that felt natural. But 2025 has been different. Several months of not socialising, not making plans, not reaching out. This isn't isolation born from fear—*it's solitude born from discovery*. The difference matters.

Grief once taught me to fear being alone because being alone meant facing the absence. But now I'm learning there's a difference between *loneliness* and *solitude.*

Loneliness is the panic, the terror, the certainty that being alone means I'm unsafe.

Solitude is this—my bed, my writing, my quiet, and the slow realisation that I'm okay here.

Taking notes has become my anchor. Not journaling—I'm a note taker. Thoughts, fragments, observations captured without pressure or performance. This entire book began as scattered notes across my phone and journals. Writing without agenda steadies me in ways nothing else can now.

I'm also learning a truth most people don't want to hear: *I give with expectations.*
People say "give without expecting anything back," but I'm calling that out. I don't keep a scorecard. I don't help friends thinking they owe me. But friendships are investments. When I go above and beyond—showing up, checking in, putting people first whilst neglecting myself—I'm not consciously expecting return. But when I need someone and they're nowhere to be found, I can't help but reflect: *I was there for you. Over and over. Where are you now?*

Some will say nobody asked me to do all those things—and they're right. I chose to be overly caring. I chose to pour myself out. I'm a natural lover, carer, giver. But that doesn't erase the imbalance when they can't meet me even halfway.

I've never met anyone who gives love the way I do. So I've learned to meet people where they actually meet me. I give less now. I protect more. My expectations have dropped so low that disappointment rarely reaches me anymore.

When 2026 begins, I'm entering it as someone rediscovered—someone who doesn't need to make plans with friends or seek new connections just to feel alive.

2026 is about going deeper: meditation, yoga, breathwork, mantras. Spiritual practices that aren't performative but genuine. Retreats where I can be one with nature—not to escape, but to finally come home to myself.

I thought I knew what *self-love* was—the gym, travel, surface-level care. But 2025 taught me that what I'd been practising was *superficial self-love*—the kind that looks good from the outside.

Now I'm discovering what self-love actually means when no one's watching—the unglamorous, unsexy, deeply necessary kind that chooses *rest over productivity, boundaries over people-pleasing, and solitude over performance.*

I love my bed. I love my quiet.
I love the version of myself I'm meeting in these still moments.

This is the work.
And for the first time in thirteen years, *I'm ready for it.*

The Art of Becoming

"You are not broken; you are becoming."

If you are reading this and you feel shattered, know this: you are not broken.

You are grieving. And grief is not damage—it is transformation.

You are not too much. You are not too sensitive. You are not failing because you cannot *"get over it"* as quickly as others think you should.

You are simply human—loving deeply, feeling fully, carrying a weight that only you can see.

And that makes you brave, not weak.

The world will move on faster than you are ready for.
People will expect you to return to "normal" long before you feel capable.

They will grow tired of your sadness, frustrated by your absence, confused by your ongoing struggle.

Let them be confused.

You do not owe anyone a performance of healing you do not feel.

Your grief is as unique as your love—as intricate, as personal, as holy.

And however you carry it, you are doing it right.

Because even in your trembling, you are still choosing to live.

Even in your silence, you are still speaking love.
Even in your survival, you are still honouring what was lost.

And that—that quiet, unseen courage—is what survives in us.

No Ending, Only Becoming

"Grief is not the end of love. It is love continuing in a new form."

This isn't the end of my grief story. It's simply where I am now—thirteen years later—still learning, still evolving, still discovering what it means to live with loss.

I don't have all the answers. I don't have a roadmap to healing that fits everyone. I only have my truth: that grief is lifelong, that love is stronger than death, and that survival—quiet, unglamorous survival—is its own kind of victory.

If you're in the early days of loss, hear me when I say this: it won't always feel this unbearable. The intensity will shift. The sharpness will dull. You'll learn to breathe around it. But it will never fully leave—and that's okay. Missing them is not a wound to cure; it's proof that they were here, that they mattered, that their love shaped you in ways that will never fade.

Grief taught me that I am stronger than I believed, more resilient than I imagined, and capable of carrying love forward even when the person is gone.

It taught me that rest is sacred. That boundaries protect peace. That saying no can be an act of survival.

It taught me that some relationships will fall away under the weight of your becoming—and that is not your fault.

It taught me that joy and sorrow can coexist. That choosing life is not betrayal; it is continuation.

Most of all, grief taught me this: love does not end. It only changes form.

I am still here. Still breathing. Still building. Still loving.

And so are you.

We are what survives.

"Grief is not the end of love. It is love continuing in a new form. And as long as I carry her memory, she is never truly gone."

COMPANION TOOLS

Sometimes grief feels too heavy for words alone.

These pages are not extra chapters. They are practical companions you can carry with you: tools to help you map your grief and to help others find their way to you.

The Grief Compass

"Grief doesn't move in straight lines. It circles, cycles, and returns."

For years, I thought I was failing because I couldn't explain what I was feeling. Sometimes sad, sometimes anger, sometimes withdrawn, sometimes heavy, sometimes crying without warning. Then I thought: I track my period each month. Why not my grief too?

I wanted to see how it visited me each year, what cycles repeated, what soft seasons surprised me. That's how The Grief Compass was born.

It is not a gratitude journal. It is not about forcing positivity. It is a place to record how grief truly shows up: the tears, the withdrawal, the silence, the anger, the numbness, the missed birthdays, the passions that disappear, the confusion about who you are now.

This is not about fixing grief. It is about naming it, so it does not quietly name you.

How I Track My Grief

I keep a simple note on my phone or in a journal. When grief shows up, I record the date and what I'm feeling. Sometimes it's just one word: *heavy. Numb. Angry*. Other times it's a full paragraph about what triggered it or where I felt it most.

I track patterns. November is always hard. The week before her birthday, I withdraw. Certain songs send me spiralling. Seeing mothers and daughters together in public still catches my breath.

The categories I notice most:

Physical: Heavy. Tired. Anxious. Flat.

Emotional: Sad. Angry. Numb. Teary.

Behavioural: Withdrawn. Isolated. Ignoring messages. Avoiding dates.

Identity: Confused. Lost passion. Don't know who I am anymore.

Every mood I record is proof I'm still here. Survival itself is a form of strength.

If you want to create your own Grief Compass, use whatever format works for you. A notes app. A journal. Voice memos. There is no wrong way. The point is simply to witness your grief, to see its patterns, to know you're not imagining how it moves through you.

A downloadable template will be available through the SayItKit. Join the waitlist at linktr.ee/elohopods

The Compassion Guide

"This is not a rulebook. It is a guide for connection."

Grief can make communication hard. Friends want to help but often don't know how, and I rarely had the energy to explain. When I was deep in grief, I wished I could hand people a simple guide: "Here is how you can show up for me right now." I didn't have the words. I didn't have the energy. And so, sometimes, we drifted apart—not because anyone didn't care, but because neither of us knew how to bridge the gap.

Grief isolates even the closest hearts. Having a way to show up changed everything for me.

Pause and reflect: How do you wish people could meet you when you feel low?

Years later, I created what I wish I'd had: a straightforward way to share what support actually feels like in the moment.

It isn't complicated. It is about presence, attention, and understanding without expectation.

What Experience Taught Me: Clarity about my needs helped others show up more effectively.

Pause and reflect: How could clarity about your needs help others show up for you?

If I Could Have Told Them Then

I could handle short texts, but not phone calls. I didn't always reply immediately, or at all on some days. That didn't mean I didn't care—it meant I was surviving.

Patience is love. Silence is not distance.

The best way to check in for me was to text first. Not just show up. Not call without warning. I needed to choose when to engage.

Pause and reflect: How can others respect your pace and space?

When I went quiet, it didn't mean I was done with anyone. It meant I was in a low place. I appreciated when people kept the door open, returned after a week or two, and didn't disappear because I withdrew first.

Let me meet you where I am, not where you hope I'll be.

What Experience Taught Me: Consistency matters more than grand gestures. Return, even when I withdraw.

Pause and reflect: How would you like people to respond when you need quiet?

Words that helped me: "Thinking of you." "Here if you need me." "I've got you." That was all. No advice. No fixing. Just presence.

What Experience Taught Me: Small words, steady presence—these become anchors in the storm.

Pause and reflect: Which words or gestures feel like a lifeline to you?

What Help Looks Like for Me

Sit with me quietly. Send a short message to say you're thinking of me. Offer gentle distractions—a walk, a cup of tea, or a glass of wine. Light conversation is welcome if I'm ready. Listen without trying to fix anything. Respect my need for space and solitude.

What Experience Taught Me: Actions without expectation speak louder than words. Simplicity is everything.

Pause and reflect: What practical support would truly help you right now?

The Days That Still Hold Weight

Her birthday. The anniversary of her death. Mother's Day. Christmas. These days carry weight for me every year. I don't pay attention to the funeral date—it wasn't something I wanted to hold in my memory, and I'm okay with that. Being remembered in ways that feel meaningful is what matters most.

But there are also times when I don't want anyone to acknowledge those days. Grief is unpredictable like that. No one's a mind reader, and people mean well, but there are moments when a message feels too heavy to receive. On those days, I might ignore it or reply later—not out of unkindness, but out of self-protection.

What Experience Taught Me: Memory carries weight, and acknowledgement softens it. Being remembered is love.

Pause and reflect: Which dates, moments, or memories matter most for your support?

What helps me whilst I'm grieving is thinking about what I actually need—not what I think I should need. When I could, I told one or two people. I wrote it down. Texted it. Emailed it. I didn't have to say it perfectly. I didn't have to share it with everyone. But giving someone specific ways to support me changed everything.

What Experience Taught Me: Clarity for myself brought clarity for others. Naming my needs became a radical act of care.

Pause and reflect: How can you begin naming your needs today, even in small ways?

This template will also be available through the SayItKit. I use this as my guide, and you can, too. Share it with those who matter, and let it help bridge the silence.

The Power of Presence

"Love is shown in presence, in listening, and in the quiet spaces between words."

Edition Notes

This is Edition One of a larger journey. Grief is not finished in one chapter, one year, or even one lifetime, and neither is this work.

There will be more:

A journal for when you want to write back to your grief

Cue cards you can keep close for sleepless nights or sudden waves

An audio companion, so these words can sit with you in the dark when reading feels too heavy

Future editions with more voices, more truths, and more lived experiences

If you purchased this book, your name is part of this circle. In the future, I will host physical meetups and dinners for readers: spaces to share stories, sit together in honesty, and eat without pretending we are fine. Because sometimes what you need most is not advice, but company.

This will grow into a community where grief is not hidden but honoured. A place where we remember together, speak our loved ones' names freely, and hold one another up when the world goes quiet.

If this book sat beside you in even one lonely hour, then it has done its work. And if you want to be part of Edition Two, sharing your story or your words, there will be space for you.

Because grief does not end. And neither does the need for companions along the way.

Stay connected:

- Eloho Uncensored Pods—https://linktr.ee/elohookumo
- SayItKit—Join the waitlist

For Those Who Are Grieving

Your anger is valid.
Your confusion is valid.
Your withdrawal is valid.
Your silence is valid.

Not replying to messages for weeks? Valid.
Not wanting to socialise? Valid.
Not knowing what you want anymore? Valid.

Losing passion for your career, your hobbies, your old life. Feeling like you're going crazy. Smiling one moment, breaking the next. All of it—valid.

There is no right way to do this. There is no timeline. There is no performance.

And here's something I wish someone had told me: you are allowed to tell people what you need. You are allowed to say "I don't want to speak right now." You are allowed to say "Don't message me for a month, I'm okay, I'm just grieving." You are allowed to set boundaries, even when it feels impossible.

Find the courage, when you can, to teach people how to be there for you. Not everyone will understand. But the ones who do, the ones who listen—they will be your anchors.

Your grief is yours. Carry it however you need to. And know that everything you're feeling right now is exactly what you're supposed to be feeling.

You are not broken. You are grieving. And that is enough.

For Those Who Love Someone Grieving

If you are reading this to understand someone you love, here is the truth I learned: they cannot be fixed. But they can be held.

Grief isolated me. It convinced me I was too much, too broken, too heavy for anyone to bear. The people who stayed—imperfect, uncertain, even clumsy—mattered more than they knew.

What Helped Me Survive

The friends who showed up consistently, not perfectly. The ones who texted even when I didn't reply. The ones who called even when I had nothing to say. "I'm thinking of you" was enough. I didn't need grand gestures. I needed to know I hadn't been forgotten.

The people who gave me permission to be quiet. Who sat with me without demanding conversation. Who understood that silence wasn't rejection—it was survival.

The specific offers. Not "Let me know if you need anything," but "I'm bringing dinner Tuesday. What time works?" I didn't have the energy to ask for help. I needed people to just do it.

The ones who were patient with my timeline. Thirteen years later, I'm still grieving. There was no deadline. The people who stopped asking when I'd "move on" were the ones who truly understood.

The ones who gave me space for my anger. I snapped. I pushed people away. The ones who stayed anyway—who understood it wasn't about them—were the ones who saved me.

What Made It Harder

When people told me I needed to move on, as if grief had an expiration date. "It's been a long time now"—as if there was a timeline I'd failed to meet.

When people said "Everything happens for a reason." These words, however well-intentioned, wounded more than they healed.

When people misunderstood my grief. When I tried to express how losing my mum affected the quality of my life, some heard it as me diminishing their problems or saying I was the only one allowed to struggle. That distance—that misunderstanding—hurt deeply.

When people disappeared because my grief made them uncomfortable. Their discomfort was temporary. My grief was not.

What I Learned About Love After Loss

People got it wrong sometimes. They said clumsy things. They offered help I couldn't accept. But the ones who tried, who stayed—they were everything.

And here's what I wish I'd known earlier: sometimes people aren't being malicious. They just don't know how to love someone through grief. They need to be told. They need permission to get it wrong. They need guidance.

If you're grieving, finding the courage to tell people what you need—even when it feels impossible—can change everything. "Don't message me for two months, I'm okay, I'm just grieving." "I don't want to talk right now." "Just sit with me in silence." It's okay to set those boundaries. It's okay to teach people how to be there for you.

If you're reading this to support someone you love, you're already doing something right. Keep reading. Keep learning. Then just show up, imperfectly but persistently.

Because love after loss doesn't need to be perfect. It just needs to be present.

Grief Comes Full Circle

As I was finalising this book, my dear Tawa—my family friend who once held me through my own loss—lost her husband suddenly.

When Jenny called me in the middle of work to tell me, everything stopped. It was the first time since losing my mum that I'd received a call like that. The kind that makes the ground give way beneath you. The kind where you hear words but can't make them real.

Since my mum died, I've walked beside grief. Three of my close friends have lost their mothers. I understand that death comes for all of us eventually—but this felt different.

This wasn't just walking beside someone else's grief. This was grief arriving at my own door again, knocking the breath out of me. If it's affecting me this deeply, can you imagine how Tawa is feeling?

Her husband was young, active, healthy—the kind of man who lit up a room and made everyone feel seen. He was about to go on holiday, and I'd told Tawa I would come stay with her for a few days whilst he was away.

On the train to see her, my cousins said something that stayed with me: *"It's because he's family. This is someone you know. Someone whose laughter you've heard, whose presence you've felt, whose home you've been in."* They were right. I'd witnessed their family dynamic. The love between Tawa, her husband, and their two boys—a rare kind of love in this modern day.

This grief is touching parts of me I didn't know were still tender.

Tawa is the person I wrote about earlier in these pages—my anchor. My quiet counsellor who let me follow her to work after my mum died so I wouldn't sit alone with spiralling thoughts. The steady presence who created structure when my world felt like chaos. She never rushed me or tried to fix me. She just held space while I fell apart.

She's also the one who once shared her fear of loss—the dread of one day having to say goodbye. She knew the ache of anticipatory grief, even while her loved ones were still here. Tawa was the first person who ever spoke to me about that fear—the fear of losing someone before you've even lost them. Her honesty stayed with me. It became the heartbeat of Chapter 12, where I wrote about loving in advance.

And now that fear has become her reality.

How is she going to survive this? Someone who already carried the fear of losing someone she loves, and now it's happening in real time. I don't have answers. But I know, from my thirteen years of living with grief, that this harsh, cruel pain will, in time, transform. It won't disappear, but it will change—sometimes quieter, sometimes louder, and in some strange way, even beautiful.

Seeing her in those first days—the shock in her eyes, the disbelief, the confusion—reminded me of something I know but am feeling all over again: grief doesn't ask for permission. It doesn't ask if you're ready. It just arrives, and life as you knew it ends in an instant.

This is why I urge you to love people whilst they're here.

Speak the words you're holding back.
Live fully. Hold no grudges.
Do the things you want to do now—not someday.

Life is too short to wait. Too fragile to take for granted.

When someone leaves, you're left holding not just their absence, but the weight of everything you didn't say, didn't do, didn't experience together. So live now. Love now. Laugh now. Forgive now. Travel. Create. Feel everything deeply—while you still can.

One day, grief will find you. And when it does, the only comfort you'll have is knowing you lived fully whilst love was still here.

Now I get to be for Tawa what she once was for me. I show up. I sit in silence. I hold space without trying to fix anything.
Grief has come full circle.

And all I can do is love her the way she loved me—steadily, gently, without expectation.

Because that's what we do. We hold each other. We show up. Even when it's hard. Especially when it's hard.

I'm so sorry, Tawa. I wish this wasn't happening to you.

The sleepless nights have returned, and I wonder when I'll find my way back to peace. But for now, I sit with this. I sit with you.

And grief doesn't ask permission before it shows up everywhere else.

This week, I've cried three times at my desk. Not because of Tawa directly, but because of everything her loss has stirred up. Normally, handling escalated client calls doesn't shake me. But lately, the smallest bit of rudeness cuts too deep. I give empathy I don't have, apologise when my heart's somewhere else, and listen to anger that feels unbearable.

Twice, I've hung up mid-call—tears threatening, patience gone—and emailed afterwards, pretending it was a technical glitch. I couldn't face calling them back. I just sat there, crying into my hands, whispering to myself: *Who has empathy left to give?* These are people upset about things that can be fixed in minutes, while I'm trying to survive something that can't be fixed at all. I'm showing compassion I can't even find for myself, and still, it isn't enough.

This is what secondary grief does. It doesn't just live in the big moments—it seeps into patience, into work, into your ability to care about things that used to matter. It reminds you that you're not fine, even when you're pretending to be.

And when peace returns, we'll find it together.

———

Grief is never still. It keeps moving—through us, around us, between us. What once broke us becomes what binds us.

This isn't just about loss. It's about love finding its way back, again and again, in new forms. It's the circle that keeps us human—the reminder that even through heartbreak, we are still connected.

And when peace finally comes, may it find us still holding each other.

For Those Who Fear Loss

If you are reading this and the person you fear losing is still here, still breathing, still calling your name, you might feel strange holding this book. You might wonder if you are being morbid, pessimistic, or inviting tragedy by acknowledging the inevitable.

You are not.

What you are feeling is anticipatory grief, and it is as real as the grief that arrives after loss. The difference is that anticipatory grief lives in silence. Society has language for mourning the dead. It has rituals for funerals, sympathy cards for the bereaved, and permission to cry when someone has gone. But there is no card that says, "I am terrified my mum will die," no socially acceptable way to say, "I lie awake imagining the day I lose them."

And the fear is not always about old age or illness. Sometimes it is simply the knowledge that life is fragile. That anyone you love—your parent, your partner, your sibling, your best friend—could be gone tomorrow. That death does not wait for grey hair or hospital beds. The fear can arrive suddenly, triggered by nothing, or by everything: a near-miss on the road, a friend's sudden loss, a news story that hits too close to home.

So you carry it quietly. You watch them grow older, slower, frailer. Or you watch them perfectly healthy today, and still feel the terror of imagining them gone. You notice the grey in their hair, the way they forget small things, the slight tremor in their hands. And each small sign feels like a countdown you cannot stop. You scroll past tributes on social media, watch friends bury their parents or lose partners unexpectedly, and think: my turn is coming. How will I survive it? Will I be the one planning the funeral? Will I fall apart? Will I be alone?

This fear is not weakness. It is love bracing itself for what it knows is inevitable.

The Quiet Loneliness of Anticipatory Grief

One of the hardest parts of anticipatory grief is that you cannot talk about it freely. If you mention your fear to the person you are afraid of losing, you risk upsetting them or making them feel like a burden. If you speak about it to others, you risk sounding dramatic or being told, "Don't think like that," as if pretending will protect you from reality.

So you stay silent. And in that silence, the fear grows heavier.

What I have observed, particularly amongst those who have never experienced deep loss, is this: if you have friends who have lost a parent, you are more likely to open up about your own fear. Watching someone else survive what you dread gives you permission to name it. You see their grief and think, will I be strong enough when my time comes? You finally have someone who will not dismiss your fear as irrational.

But if you have not yet witnessed close loss, the fear can feel isolating. You carry it alone, wondering if you are the only one lying awake rehearsing a future you cannot control.

You are not alone. Millions of people carry this same quiet dread. They simply do not speak it aloud.

How It Differs from Grief After Loss

Anticipatory grief is complicated because the person is still here. You are mourning whilst they are still alive, which can feel like a betrayal. You might feel guilty for thinking about their death whilst they are sitting across from you at dinner. You might feel ashamed for planning what you would do after they are gone, as though imagining it will somehow make it happen sooner.

The fear might be about watching them age or decline from illness. Or it might be about the randomness of life—the knowledge that a car accident, a sudden illness, or an unexpected tragedy could take them at any moment. Either way, the weight is the same: you are carrying the awareness of mortality whilst they are still here.

But preparing for loss is not the same as wishing for it. Anticipatory grief does not mean you love them less. It means you love them so much that the thought of a world without them is unbearable.

After loss, grief is about absence. You are learning to live in a world where they no longer exist. Anticipatory grief is about presence laced with fear. You are trying to live fully with them now whilst carrying the knowledge that one day, you will not be able to.

The challenge is this: how do you prepare your heart without letting fear steal the joy of today?

Learning to Live in the Tension

Anticipatory grief asks you to hold two truths at once:

- They are here now, and I can still hold them, hear them, love them.
- One day, they will not be here, and I need to prepare myself for that reality.

This tension is exhausting. It means being present whilst also being vigilant. It means savouring moments whilst simultaneously feeling the ache of their impermanence.

Some days, you will manage this well. You will laugh with them, film them and record their voice, ask the questions you have been holding back. Other days, the weight of future loss will press so heavily that you cannot enjoy their presence at all. You will look at them and see only the ghost of their absence.

Be gentle with yourself on those days. You are carrying something heavy, and it is understandable that sometimes it is too much to bear gracefully.

If You're Reading Before Loss

If you are reading this before loss has arrived, you have something precious: time. Time to gather what will matter later. Time to say the words you might otherwise leave unsaid. Time to create an archive of love that will hold you when grief finally comes.

Chapter 12 offers practical guidance on what to save and how to speak before it is too late. But beyond the practical, I want you to know this: your fear is not a curse. It is clarity. Most people are blindsided by loss. They do not see it coming, and the shock compounds the grief. You, however, are awake to the reality of impermanence. That awareness, though painful, is also a gift.

Use it wisely. Let it guide you towards presence rather than paralysis. Let it remind you to love them loudly whilst you still can.

If you want to understand what people wish they had done differently after loss, read Chapter 14 on regret whilst you still have time to act. Those stories are not meant to haunt you but to guide you. They are lessons from those of us who did not know we were running out of time.

What I Know Now

When I lost my mum at twenty-two, I was just living my best life. I had no warning, no preparation, no sense that time was running out. She died suddenly. Vibrant one day, gone the next. I thought I had decades to ask her questions, to learn her recipes, to record her laugh, to tell her I loved her more often. I assumed tomorrow was guaranteed.

It was not.

Loss does not always come with warnings. It does not always give you time to prepare. Sometimes it arrives suddenly, shattering everything in an instant. And when it does, you are left holding not only grief but also the weight of everything you didn't say, didn't ask, didn't save.

As you grow older and experience life more deeply, you come to understand that loss is not an "if" but a "when." We all know, somewhere in the back of our minds, that we will lose the people we love. But knowing this intellectually and preparing for it emotionally are two different things.

If I had known then what I know now, I would have done things differently. I would have filmed more often and pressed record more. I would have asked harder questions. I would have taken more photos, cooked more meals together, travelled more, laughed louder. I would have made sure she knew, every single day, how deeply I loved her.

I cannot go back and do those things. But you can. You still have time. And that is why I am writing this to you now.

How to Carry Less Regret Later

Everyone who experiences deep loss carries regrets. It is almost universal. The regret of words left unsaid, questions left unasked, time left unshared. The regret of assuming there would be more birthdays, more holidays, more ordinary Tuesday afternoons.

Most regrets come from two things: lack of preparation and the false belief that you have more time.

But you are reading this book. You are thinking about loss before it arrives. You are already doing something most people do not do until it is too late. And that means you have the power to reduce your future regrets significantly.

Will you still have some regrets when they are gone? Yes. Grief almost always carries a measure of "I wish I had." But those regrets might be lighter if you act now. If you tell them you love them. If you film them and record their voice. If you ask the questions. If you create the memories. If you travel together, cook their favourite dishes together, laugh out loud together.

These moments are not just for today. They are investments in your future self. When grief comes, you will reach for these memories like treasure. And you will be so grateful that you did not wait.

The Conversations That Feel Heavy—But Matter

Part of preparing for loss means having conversations that feel uncomfortable. It means asking questions that might make both of you squirm a little. But these conversations are acts of love, not morbidity.

If you feel ready, you might gently ask: How would you like to be remembered? How would you like to be buried or cremated? What kind of funeral would feel true to you? These questions feel heavy because they acknowledge mortality. But they can also be gifts. One day, you may be the person making these decisions, and knowing their wishes might bring you some peace when everything else feels chaotic.

I can say confidently now that I want to be cremated when I die. I can talk about this openly because I have experienced deep loss, and I know how much it would have helped to know my mum's wishes. If she were still here, I would ask her. And I encourage you to find a gentle, loving way to ask the people you love whilst you still can.

It might feel awkward at first. But most people, when given the space, are willing to share these thoughts. And having that conversation now might ease some of the uncertainty and guilt when the time comes.

SayItKit: Your Guide for This Journey

This is where tools like the SayItKit become more than paper and prompts. They become an investment in your future.

The SayItKit helps you:

- Write the Forever Letter: the words you want them to have, and the words you want to capture from them
- Film and record their voice, their laugh, their stories before silence arrives
- Ask the questions you have been holding back
- Gather the recipes, the family histories, the small details that feel ordinary now but will become treasures later
- Create a living archive of love that will hold you when they are gone

Every letter written, every video captured, every voice recorded, every memory sealed is something you can hold when the silence finally arrives. The Legacy Letter section of the SayItKit, and the Forever Voices idea, are designed exactly for this: to help you create a living archive of love.

This is not just preparation. This is an act of love. For them, and for your future self.

You Are Not Morbid—You Are Awake

If someone has made you feel strange for thinking about death, for wanting to prepare, for reading a book about grief before you are grieving, let me say this clearly: you are not morbid. You are realistic. You are brave. You are doing something most people avoid until it is too late.

Loss is not an "if." It is a "when." Everyone with living parents, partners, siblings, or friends will one day face this. Preparing your heart for that reality is not inviting tragedy. It is being honest about the nature of life and love.

Finding the Ones Who Understand

If you are carrying this fear, seek out others who understand. This might mean friends who have already lost someone and can hold space for your fear without dismissing it. It might mean a therapist who specialises in anticipatory grief. It might mean online communities where people speak openly about preparing for loss.

You do not have to carry this alone. And you do not have to wait until after loss to seek support.

A Final Word

One day, the fear you carry now will become the grief you read about in the earlier chapters of this book. When that day comes—whether it arrives gradually or suddenly, whether you lose a parent, a partner, a sibling, or a friend—you will return to these pages differently. You will no longer be preparing. You will be surviving.

But until then, you are here. *They are* here. And that is enough.

If you can—love them now. Tell them now. Film them now. Record them now. Cook with them now. Travel with them now. Laugh out loud with them now. Ask all the questions you are holding back—the ones you keep saying, *"Oh, don't worry, I'll learn that tomorrow."*

What if you didn't wait for tomorrow? What if you learned your mum's favourite dish today, asked about their childhood today, took the photos today, filmed the ordinary moments today?

This is your investment. This is your treasure. *SayItKit* will help guide you through this process, but the most important tool you have is time. And you still have it.

When grief finally arrives, you will carry not only loss but also the treasures you chose to gather whilst love was still within reach.

You will still have regrets. But they might be lighter. You will still have pain. But it might be softer—because you loved them loudly whilst you could.

You are not alone in this fear. And you will not be alone in the grief that follows.

But for now, they are here. So if you can—speak. Film them. Record their voice. Love them loudly. Ask what you've been holding back. Do what you can, whilst you still can.

Love. Ask. Create. Travel. Laugh. Save.

Time is short

You still have time to love them in ways your future self will thank you for.

Afterword: The Final Note

If you have reached this page, pause and give yourself credit. You have faced one of the hardest journeys a person can undertake—and you are here.

This book was never meant to be a cure. It was meant to be the friend I desperately needed at twenty-two: the voice that said, "That confusion is normal. That fear is grief. You are not going crazy, and you are absolutely not alone."

And even now, it remains a companion I still turn to—a reminder that no matter how much time passes, we still need gentle words to hold us through what never fully leaves us.

The sleepless nights may still return. The silence may still feel too loud. When that happens, remember this: the chaos you experience is simply the energy of a profound love that has nowhere left to go but into the rest of your life.

If you're wondering where I am now, in 2025, here's the truth: I'm still learning.

Therapy is next—not because I'm healed, but because I've realised this second season of grief needs different tools than the first.

The paralysis hasn't completely lifted, but the podcast, this book, and the SayItKit have given me small anchors: projects to build toward when everything else feels uncertain. Some weeks I feel momentum. Other weeks, I feel stuck. Both are okay.

With Tony, words linger—paused somewhere between us, yet somehow still reaching across the quiet. With Timi, a quiet thread hums its way home, steady enough to be felt. Love endures. Silence may settle. *But connection remains.*

I'm still here in London, still figuring out what purpose looks like when ambition hasn't fully returned. But I'm here. That counts. And on the days when being here feels too much, I remind myself: survival is the work. Everything else is extra.

The work now is to channel that love. Use the SayItKit with the people you still have. Find the rituals that hold you every time the calendar threatens to pull you back. Let your survival become your purpose.

Your grief will always be a companion, but it does not have to be a commander. I am the architect of my reconstruction, and the love I carry for her will always be my greatest anchor.

Now take a deep breath. Look around at the life you've fought so hard to build. The journey is not over.

From my own experience, I've learned this: the love will never leave. The love I carry for her—it will always be my companion.

Acknowledgements

To my mum: Everything I am, everything I've survived, everything I've built—it all comes back to you. You are my God, my rock, my compass. I carry you in every breath, every choice, every moment. This book is my way of keeping your love visible in a world that no longer holds you. I miss you every single day.

To my brothers, Timi and Tony: We lost the same woman, but we each carried her absence differently. I hope one day we find the courage to share those stories together. Until then, know that I see your grief, even in the silence, and that we are forever bound by the same extraordinary love.

To my friends mentioned in this book: thank you for showing up in the ways you could—for being part of the story that held me together when I was falling apart.

To the friends not directly named: you are not forgotten. If you were in my life, your presence had impact, your love made a difference, and your care helped me survive.

To my newer friends: thank you for arriving in the later chapters of my life, for holding me in seasons when grief had already reshaped me, and for meeting me where I was instead of where I used to be.

To the friendships that could not withstand the weight of loss: I carry no bitterness. Your absence, too, became part of grief's lesson—that not every relationship survives, but every one leaves something behind.

To my podcast community: thank you for giving voice to grief with me, for trusting me with your stories, and for helping transform silence into conversation.

To the incredible guests who shared their stories, and to the counsellor and psychotherapist who guided so many of those conversations: your wisdom, care, and insight have shaped not only the podcast but also this book. Without you, this work would not have been possible.

And to you, the reader: thank you for choosing to sit with me in these dark hours. Thank you for trusting these words to meet you in your pain. I hope this book has been a companion—a reminder of this simple truth: you are not alone. You never were.

Resources & Next Steps

When the book closes, the real work continues. If you are struggling to maintain your equilibrium, please use the following resources and tools built to help you survive the dark hours.

Stay Connected: The Toolkit & Community

eloho Uncensored Pods: You are invited to join the conversation. The podcast is a space where the silence ends, and we explore the raw, unfiltered realities of grief and healing, and human connection.

Visit: https://linktr.ee/elohookumo

SayItKit: This is the practical tool born from the regret of the unsaid. Use it to help you practise saying the loving, difficult, or necessary words to those in your life, whilst there is still time.

Join the waitlist: https://linktr.ee/elohookumo

Professional Support

Immediate Crisis

If at any point you feel unsafe, unable to cope, or in crisis, please reach out immediately for support.

- **United Kingdom**: Call Samaritans at 116 123 (free, 24/7)
- **United States**: Call or text 988 to connect with the Suicide & Crisis Lifeline
- **Canada**: Call or text 988 (Suicide Crisis Helpline, nationwide, 24/7)
- **South Africa**: Call SADAG Helpline at 0800 567 567 or SMS 31393 (24/7)
- **Nigeria**: Call Mentally Aware Nigeria Helpline at 0809 111 6264

- **Other African countries**: Visit findahelpline.com for local numbers
- **International**: Visit findahelpline.com to locate support anywhere in the world

Ongoing Support

This book shares personal reflections and experiences of grief. It is not a substitute for professional medical advice, diagnosis, or treatment. Please consult a qualified mental health professional (counsellor, therapist, or doctor) for personalised support.

Above all, remember: seeking help is not weakness. It is how love learns to carry you, until you can carry yourself again.

About the Author

eloho okumo turns silence into language and grief into connection.

She is a creative director, tv producer, and human communication and customer experience consultant with over a decade of experience crafting emotionally grounded storytelling across reality, documentary, and branded content. Her work centres human truth: the things people feel but rarely say.

She is the curator and host of *elohouncensoredpods,* a podcast where grief is spoken out loud, not sanitized, not softened, just honest. She turned her pain into power and hit record. She is also the creator of *SayItKit,* a reflective toolkit designed to help people find the language to say what matters most while there is still time, so love doesn't live in regret.

After losing her mother at twenty-two, eloho spent thirteen years learning how to survive before she could teach others how to heal.

Thirteen years later, she finally had the words.

Sleepless Night: A Companion for the Dark Hours is the book she desperately needed at twenty-two, still needs at thirty-six, and will reach for again whenever loss arrives. The kind of book you return to every time grief finds you.

It names what grief actually feels like: the 3am panic that feels like dying, the daytime fog where you're present but not really there, the paralysis that steals your will to move forward. It's not just about death. It's about any loss that cracks you open and leaves you wondering if you're broken.

This book doesn't just comfort those already grieving. It teaches people how to love out loud before loss arrives, turning anticipation into action. It's for three types of people: the grieving, the bracing, and the witnessing. For anyone who needs language when silence feels like drowning.

She's also created the *Companion Toolkit,* a system to help the grieving communicate their needs and train supporters how to show up. Because without tools like these, grief doesn't just break hearts. It quietly damages relationships when silence is misread as rejection.

Loss taught eloho that words matter more than we realise. That care can be coded. That efficiency can erase empathy. Now, she helps AI-driven organisations humanise customer and internal communication—ensuring efficiency never comes at the cost of care, and automation never feels cold, generic, or emotionally misaligned. She brings to the corporate world the same truth she learned in grief: communication should make people feel seen, not processed.

Her work spans documentaries, original formats, and tools for expression. Through podcasting, producing, and building spaces for difficult conversations, she creates places where silence ends, healing begins, and love is remembered.

eloho knows that grief never ends. It's a school where we're all enrolled, moving from primary to secondary to PhD, but we never graduate. We just learn to carry it differently.

And still, she misses her mum every single day.

Through every word, every project, every conversation, she's still searching for her.

"Grief cracked me open. Love poured out. So I built it a home, one that could hold us both."

—elohookumo

Companion Toolkit & Resources

This book comes with a free Companion Toolkit.

Scan the QR code below to download.

A £1 platform fee covers delivery costs.

Printed in Dunstable, United Kingdom

79149456R00139